Hydrogeologic Framework, Groundwater and Surface-Water Systems, Land Use, Pumpage, and Water Budget of the Chamokane Creek Basin, Stevens County, Washington

By Sue C. Kahle, William A. Taylor, Sonja Lin, Steven S. Sumioka, and Theresa D. Olsen

Prepared in cooperation with the Bureau of Indian Affairs and the Washington State Department of Ecology

Scientific Investigations Report 2010–5165

U.S. Department of the Interior
U.S. Geological Survey

U.S. Department of the Interior
KEN SALAZAR, Secretary

U.S. Geological Survey
Marcia K. McNutt, Director

U.S. Geological Survey, Reston, Virginia: 2010

For more information on the USGS—the Federal source for science about the Earth, its natural and living resources, natural hazards, and the environment, visit http://www.usgs.gov or call 1-888-ASK-USGS

For an overview of USGS information products, including maps, imagery, and publications, visit http://www.usgs.gov/pubprod

To order this and other USGS information products, visit http://store.usgs.gov

Suggested citation:
Kahle, S.C., Taylor, W.A., Lin, Sonja, Sumioka, S.S., and Olsen, T.D., 2010, Hydrogeologic framework, groundwater and surface-water systems, land use, pumpage, and water budget of the Chamokane Creek basin, Stevens County, Washington: U.S. Geological Survey Scientific Investigations Report 2010-5165, 60 p.

Contents

Plates

[In pocket]

Figures

Tables

Conversion Factors, Datums, Abbreviations and Acronyms, and Well- and Spring-Numbering System

Conversion Factors

Inch/Pound to SI

Multiply	By	To obtain
Length		
inch (in.)	2.54	centimeter (cm)
inch (in.)	25.4	millimeter (mm)
foot (ft)	0.3048	meter (m)
mile (mi)	1.609	kilometer (km)
Area		
acre	4,047	square meter (m^2)
square mile (mi^2)	2.590	square kilometer (km^2)
Volume		
gallon (gal)	3.785	liter (L)
gallon (gal)	0.003785	cubic meter (m^3)
million gallons (Mgal)	3,785	cubic meter (m^3)
cubic mile (mi^3)	4.168	cubic kilometer (km^3)
Flow rate		
foot per day (ft/d)	0.3048	meter per day (m/d)
cubic foot per second (ft^3/s)	0.02832	cubic meter per second (m^3/s)
cubic foot per day (ft^3/d)	0.02832	cubic meter per day (m^3/d)
gallon per minute (gal/min)	0.06309	liter per second (L/s)
gallon per day (gal/d)	0.003785	cubic meter per day (m^3/d)
gallon per year (gal/yr)	0.003785	cubic meter per day (m^3/d)

Conversion Factors, Datums, Abbreviations and Acronyms and Well- and Spring-Numbering System—Continued

Inch/Pound to SI—Continued

Multiply	By	To obtain
million gallons per year (Mgal/yr)	3,785	cubic meter per year (m³/yr)
Specific capacity		
gallon per minute per foot [(gal/min)/ft]	0.2070	liter per second per meter [(L/s)/m]
Hydraulic conductivity		
foot per day (ft/d)	0.3048	meter per day
Hydraulic gradient		
foot per mile (ft/mi)	0.1894	meter per kilometer
Transmissivity*		
square foot per day (ft²/d)	0.09290	square meter per day (m²/d)

SI to Inch/Pound

Multiply	By	To obtain
Length		
meter (m)	3.281	foot (ft)
Area		
square meter (m²)	0.0002471	acre

Temperature in degrees Celsius (°C) may be converted to degrees Fahrenheit (°F) as follows:

$$°F=(1.8×°C)+32$$

*Transmissivity: The standard unit for transmissivity is cubic foot per day per square foot times foot of aquifer thickness [(ft³/d)/ft²]ft. In this report, the mathematically reduced form, foot squared per day (ft²/d), is used for convenience.

Datums

Vertical coordinate information is referenced to the North American Vertical Datum of 1988 (NAVD 88).

Horizontal coordinate information is referenced to the North American Datum of 1983 (NAD 83).

Altitude, as used in this report, refers to distance above the vertical datum.

Abbreviations and Acronyms

ANUDEM	Australian National University Digital Elevation Model
BIA	Bureau of Indian Affairs
BR	Bedrock unit
BT	Basalt unit
DEM	digital elevation model
EROS	Earth Resources Observation and Science Center
ET	evapotranspiration
GIS	Geographic Information System
LA	Lower aquifer
LU	Landslide unit
LULC	land use and land cover
Mb	Miocene basalts
MSS	multispectral scanner
NOAA	National Oceanic and Atmospheric Administration
NED	National Elevation Dataset
NWIS	National Water Information System
TM	thematic mapper
UA	Upper outwash aquifer
USDA	U.S. Department of Agriculture
USGS	U.S. Geological Survey
VC	Valley confining unit

Well- and Spring-Numbering System

In Washington, wells and springs are assigned numbers that identify their location in a township, range, section, and 40-acre tract. For example, well number 29N/40E-23M06 indicates that the well is in township 29 north of the Willamette Base Line, and range 40 east of the Willamette Meridian. The numbers immediately following the hyphen indicate the section (23) in the township, and the letter following the section (M) gives the 40-acre tract of the section. The two-digit sequence number (06) following the letter indicates that the well was the sixth one inventoried by project personnel in that 40-acre tract. A "D" following the sequence number indicates that the well has been deepened. An "S" following the sequence number indicates that the site is a spring. In the illustrations of this report, wells and springs are identified individually using only the section and 40-acre tract, such as 23M06. The townships and ranges are shown on the map borders.

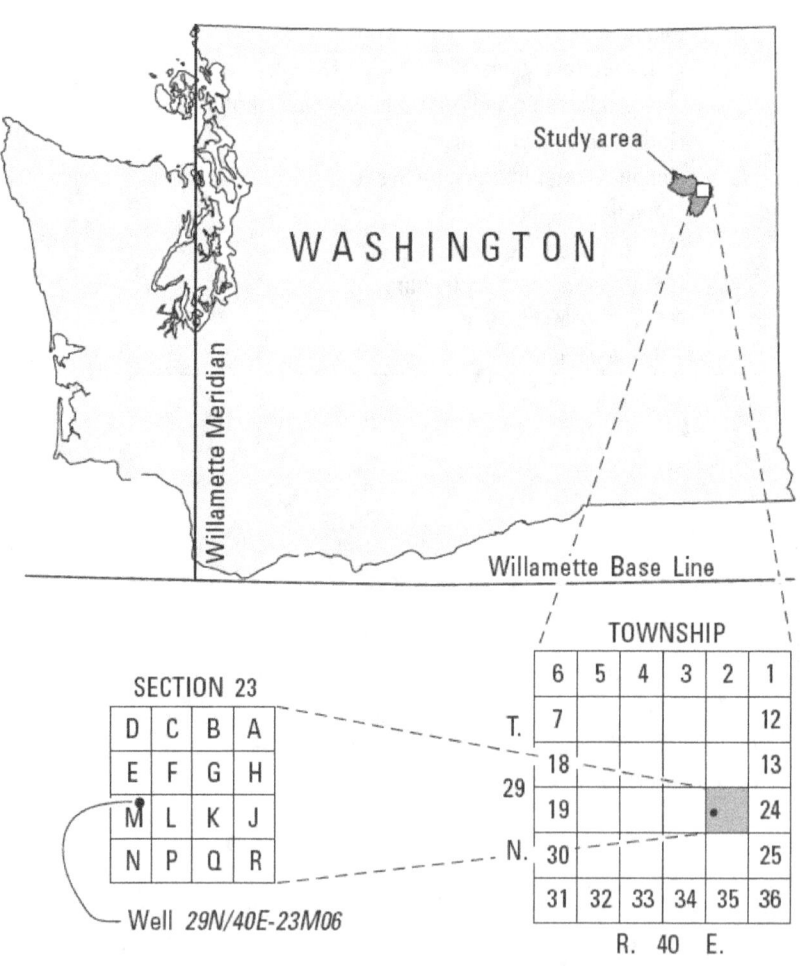

Diagram showing well numbering system in Washington

Hydrogeologic Framework, Groundwater and Surface-Water Systems, Land Use, Pumpage, and Water Budget of the Chamokane Creek Basin, Stevens County, Washington

By Sue C. Kahle, William A. Taylor, Sonja Lin, Steven S. Sumioka, and Theresa D. Olsen

Abstract

A study of the water resources of the unconsolidated groundwater system of the Chamokane Creek basin was conducted to determine the hydrogeologic framework, interactions of shallow and deep parts of the groundwater system with each other and the surface-water system, changes in land use and land cover, and water-use estimates. Chamokane Creek basin is a 179 mi^2 area that borders and partially overlaps the Spokane Indian Reservation in southern Stevens County in northeastern Washington State. Aquifers within the Chamokane Creek basin are part of a sequence of glaciofluvial and glaciolacustrine sediment that may reach total thicknesses of about 600 ft. In 1979, most of the water rights in the Chamokane Creek basin were adjudicated by the United States District Court requiring regulation in favor of the Spokane Tribe of Indians' senior water right. The Spokane Tribe, the State of Washington, and the United States are concerned about the effects of additional groundwater development within the basin on Chamokane Creek. Information provided by this study will be used to evaluate the effects of potential increases in groundwater withdrawals on groundwater and surface-water resources within the basin.

The hydrogeologic framework consists of six hydrogeologic units: The Upper outwash aquifer, the Landslide Unit, the Valley Confining Unit, the Lower Aquifer, the Basalt Unit, and the Bedrock Unit. The Upper outwash aquifer occurs along the valley floors of the study area and consists of sand, gravel, cobbles, boulders, with minor silt and (or) clay interbeds in places. The Lower aquifer is a confined aquifer consisting of sand and gravel that occurs at depth below the Valley confining unit. Median horizontal hydraulic conductivity values for the Upper outwash aquifer, Valley confining unit, Lower aquifer, and Basalt unit were estimated to be 540, 10, 19, and 3.7 ft/d, respectively.

Many low-flow stream discharge measurements at sites on Chamokane Creek and its tributaries were at or near zero flow. The most notable exception is where Chamokane Creek is supported by discharge of large springs from the Upper outwash aquifer in the southern part of the basin. Most high-flow measurements indicated gains in streamflow (groundwater discharging to the stream). Large streamflow losses, however, were recorded near the north end of Walkers Prairie where streamflow directly recharges the Upper outwash aquifer. The similarity in seasonal water-level fluctuations in the Upper outwash aquifer and the Lower aquifer indicate that these systems may be fairly well connected.

Land use and land cover change analysis indicates that Chamokane Creek basin has been dominated by forests with some pasture and agricultural lands with sparse residential development from the 1980s to present. Loss in forest cover represents the largest change in land cover in the basin between 1987 and 2009. This appears to be mostly due to forestry activities, especially in the northern part of the basin. Since 1987, more than 18,000 acres of evergreen forest have been logged and are at various stages of regrowth.

Estimated average annual total groundwater pumpage in the basin increased from 224 million gallons per year (Mgal/yr) in 1980 to 1,330 Mgal/yr in 2007. The largest withdrawals during 2007 were to supply two fish hatcheries, with a combined total annual pumpage of about 1,150 Mgal. Annual groundwater pumpage values from 1980 through 2007 for the study area ranged from 21.1 to 28.9 Mgal/yr for domestic wells and 0.38 to 23.7 Mgal/yr for public supply. An approximate water budget for a typical year in the Chamokane Creek basin indicates that 19.6 in. of precipitation are balanced by 4.7 in. of streamflow discharge from the basin, and 14.9 in. of evapotranspiration.

Introduction

Chamokane Creek basin is a 179 mi^2 area that borders and partially overlaps the Spokane Indian Reservation in southern Stevens County in northeastern Washington State (fig. 1). It is a roughly boot-shaped, northwest-to-south-trending basin about 28 mi long and 7 mi wide. Chamokane Creek flows toward the east through the Camas Valley to near the town of Springdale, Washington, where the creek turns southeast and then flows generally south through the Chamokane Valley and Walkers Prairie toward the town of

Ford, Washington. Mean September streamflow in Chamokane Creek at Chamokane Falls, as recorded at U.S. Geological Survey (USGS) streamflow-gaging station 12433200 (fig. 1), for 1971–2008 was 27 ft³/s. Aquifers in the Chamokane Creek basin are part of a sequence of glaciofluvial and glaciolacustrine sediment that may reach total thicknesses of about 600 ft. Most wells within the basin are completed in an upper unconfined aquifer or in a confined aquifer that occurs at depth beneath the Camas and Chamokane Valleys. The two aquifers are separated by a silt and clay unit that can be more than 300 ft thick and appears laterally continuous. Basalt or bedrock, consisting mostly of granite and (or) meta-sedimentary rocks, underlies the sediment at generally unknown depths.

In 1979, most of the water rights in the Chamokane Creek basin were adjudicated by the United States District Court. Since the 1979 adjudication, the District Court has issued various amendments and orders that affect water users in the basin. The Chamokane Creek Adjudication requires that junior water right holders on Chamokane Creek, and its tributaries, be regulated in favor of the more senior water right of the Spokane Tribe. This senior water right was granted as a reserved water right for irrigation and protection of the Spokane Tribe's Ancestral Fishing Rights in Chamokane Creek. A court-appointed Water Master regulates junior water rights when the mean daily 7-day low flow becomes less than 24 ft³/s (27 ft³/s for rights issued after December 1988) at Chamokane Falls, as recorded at U.S. Geological Survey (USGS) streamflow-gaging station 12433200 (fig. 1). Regulation has been necessary in 3 recent years (2001, 2005, and 2008). The non-Reservation areas of the basin are closed to any additional groundwater or surface-water appropriation, with the exception of "permit exempt" uses of groundwater. These exempt uses in Washington State do not require a water right and include stock watering, lawn or non-commercial garden watering, single or group domestic uses of as much as 5,000 gal/d, and small-scale industrial use not to exceed 5,000 gal/d (Washington State Department of Ecology, 2006).

The 1979 District Court Judgment contends that groundwater withdrawals in the Upper Chamokane region had no effect on the flow of Chamokane Creek because groundwater in the upper region was considered to be part of a separate aquifer from that in the Chamokane Valley. Despite the ruling, there are concerns about the effects of future groundwater development that may occur in the upstream end of the basin, particularly outside the reservation boundary. The relation between the upper (Camas Valley and Chamokane Creek headwaters) and lower (Chamokane Valley) Chamokane Creek basin groundwater systems has not been directly studied. With increasing population and residential development, permit exempt groundwater use is expected to continue and the potential effects of this growth on Chamokane Creek are unknown.

Finally, although the upper aquifer within the Chamokane Valley has been fairly well characterized (Wozniewicz, 1989), the hydrogeologic framework of the entire basin, as well as the nature and extent of the lower aquifer, is poorly understood. An assessment of the hydrogeologic framework of the entire basin was needed prior to an assessment of the effects of groundwater use on the surface-water system.

To evaluate these concerns and uncertainties, the USGS began a study in 2007 with the primary goals of describing the groundwater and surface-water system of the valley-fill deposits of the basin and assessing the effects of potential increases in groundwater withdrawals on groundwater and surface-water resources. The study includes an evaluation of the 1979 judgment contending that groundwater withdrawals in the upper Chamokane Creek basin do not affect Chamokane Creek.

This report describes the results from Phase 1 of a two-part study. The objectives of Phase 1 were to characterize the hydrogeologic setting and groundwater and surface-water interactions within the basin, and to obtain selected hydrologic data sets to support construction and calibration of a coupled groundwater and surface-water flow model in Phase 2. Phase 1 data collection efforts were focused on the area within and adjacent to the drainage basin boundary shown in figure 1 .

Phase 2 is currently (2010) ongoing and will build on the findings of Phase 1. Regional model boundaries will be described in Phase 2 including rationale for where the model boundaries differ from the drainage basin boundary. The objectives of Phase 2 are to build and apply a coupled groundwater and surface-water flow model using GSFLOW (Markstrom and others, 2008) to evaluate the possible regional effects of different groundwater-use scenarios on the surface-water system. The GSFLOW model also will be used to provide an estimate of recharge and a comprehensive water budget for the groundwater system. Additionally, the model will be used to further describe groundwater and surface-water interactions in the basin. Specific study objectives include:

Phase 1

1. Characterize the hydrogeologic framework of the Chamokane Creek basin;

2. Describe the groundwater and surface-water flow system within the basin; and

3. Estimate water use within the basin at the time of adjudication (1979) and present for permit exempt and non-exempt uses of groundwater and surface water.

Phase 2

1. Evaluate the contention that groundwater withdrawals in the Upper Chamokane region have no affect on flow in Chamokane Creek; and

2. Evaluate hydrologic system responses to various stresses using a coupled groundwater and surface-water flow model.

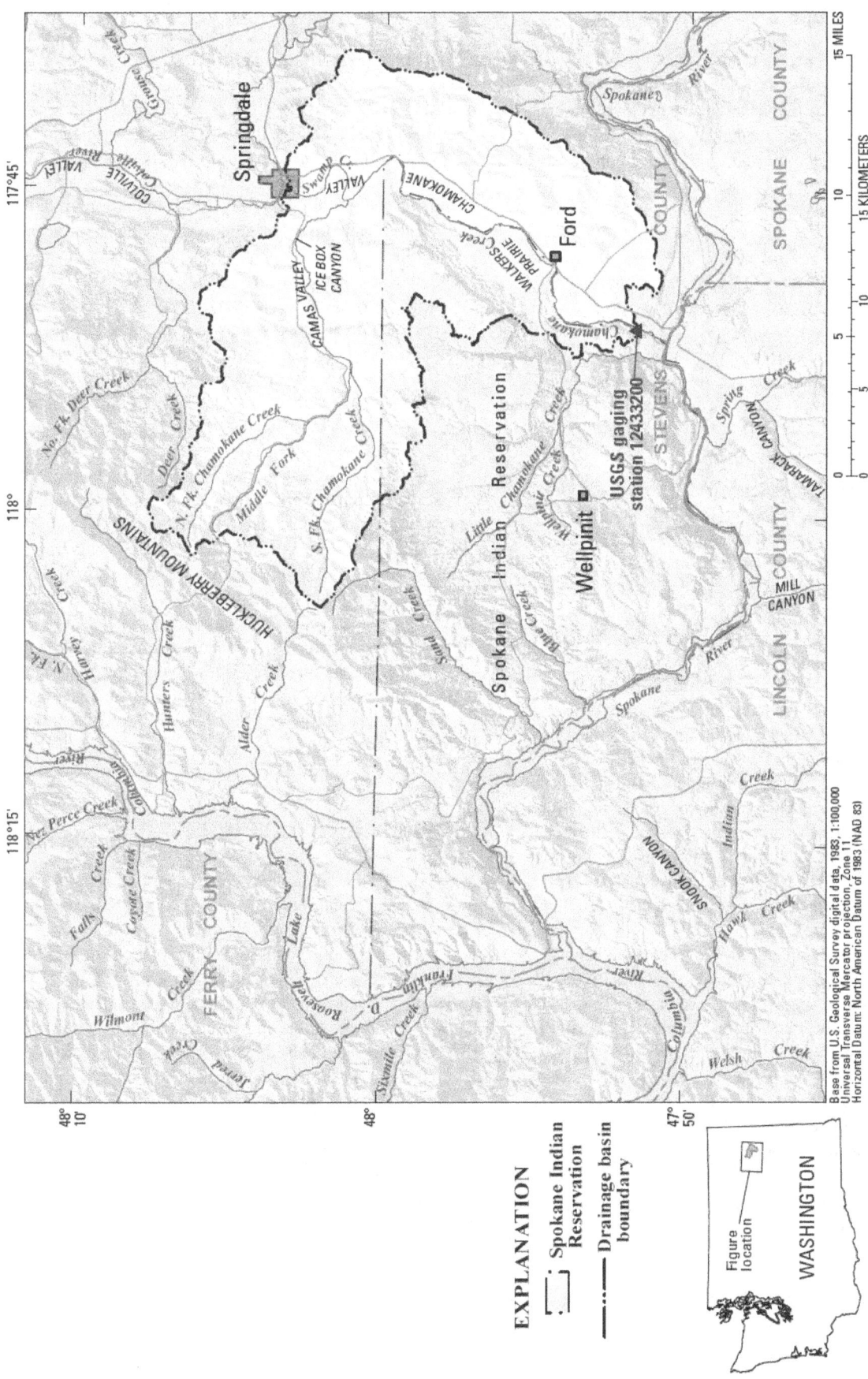

Figure 1. Location of the Chamokane Creek basin, Stevens County, Washington.

EXPLANATION

Spokane Indian Reservation

Drainage basin boundary

Base from U.S. Geological Survey digital data, 1983, 1:100,000
Universal Transverse Mercator projection, Zone 11
Horizontal Datum: North American Datum of 1983 (NAD 83)

WASHINGTON

Figure location

Purpose and Scope

This report presents the results of the Phase 1 study of the groundwater and surface-water systems in the Chamokane Creek basin. It describes the hydrogeologic framework of the basin, including the extent and thickness of significant hydrogeologic units, discusses groundwater interactions between hydrogeologic units and with the surface-water system, describes land- and water-use types, and discusses additional data needs. The scope of the report includes a description of the regional and local geologic history, the surficial geology of the basin, the physical characteristics of the hydrogeologic units, and groundwater levels and generalized flow directions. Also described are the characteristics of the streamflow network, a description of land-use types and changes over time, summaries of groundwater withdrawals within the basin, and an approximate water budget for the basin.

Description of Study Area

Chamokane Creek has its headwaters in the Huckleberry Mountains that attain elevations of about 4,600 ft. The creek flows east from its headwaters into Camas Valley, a southwest-northeast oriented valley about 6.5 mi long (fig. 1). From Camas Valley, Chamokane Creek flows through Ice Box Canyon and then southeast about 4 mi where it is slightly entrenched in a system of outwash terraces. The creek continues southeast to a bedrock outcrop where it changes course and flows southwest into Walkers Prairie where flows are intermittent. On the southern end of Walkers Prairie, a series of large springs discharge from an east-west oriented bluff west of Ford (pl. 1). Discharge from these springs and outflow from two hatcheries provides most of the perennial flow in Chamokane Creek from near Ford to the confluence with the Spokane River. Chamokane Falls is about 1.5 mi upstream of the confluence where Chamokane Creek flows over a bedrock outcrop (pl. 1).

A low elevation drainage divide near Springdale, Washington, between the north-flowing Colville River and the south-flowing Chamokane Creek is underlain by glacial outwash and till associated with the Colville sublobe of the Cordilleran ice sheet and, at greater depths, by thick clay and silt deposited in large Pleistocene lakes (Kahle and others, 2003). These unconsolidated deposits form a shallow surface-drainage divide in an otherwise broad and continuous Colville-Chamokane Valley. A pre-glacial Columbia River may have flowed southward through the present-day Colville and Chamokane Valley, resulting in the long and wide valley that is visible today (Willis, 1887; Carrara and others, 1996).

Most mountainous areas in the basin are covered with pine, fir, and larch forests that are the basis for the historical and current (2009) lumber industry in the area. In the lowland areas of the basin, agricultural land use is widespread, including grazing and hay production, along with scattered developed areas, including the town of Ford, Washington. About 34 mi^2 of the Spokane Indian Reservation lies within Chamokane Creek basin with Chamokane Creek's east bank forming the eastern border of the Reservation from just north of 48 degrees latitude to the confluence of Chamokane Creek and the Spokane River (fig. 1). Two fish hatcheries, one operated by the State and one by the Spokane Tribe, are on the north side of Chamokane Creek west of Ford (pl. 1). An inactive uranium ore processing site, owned by Dawn Mining Company, is on 820 acres south of Ford (pl. 1). Ore was processed at the site from 1956 to 1982; cleanup at the site continues with oversight provided by the Washington State Department of Health (http://www.doh.wa.gov/ehp/rp/waste/dmchm.htm, accessed January 5, 2010).

The climate in the study area varies from subhumid to semiarid and is characterized by warm, dry summers and cool, moist winters (Molenaar, 1988). The mean annual (1923–2007) precipitation value for the nearest long-term weather station in Wellpinit, Wash. is 18.95 in. (http://www.wrcc.dri.edu/cgi-bin/cliMAIN.pl?wa9058, accessed January 6, 2010). Historically, most precipitation falls as snow during the 5-month period from November through March. Average annual precipitation for 1971–2000 varies from a minimum of about 14 in. at the southern edge to more than 25 in. in the northernmost headwaters of the basin (Western Regional Climate Center, 2010) (fig. 2).

Previous Investigations

Previous investigations that have contributed to the understanding of the water resources in the Chamokane Creek basin generally fall in one of three categories. The first category includes small-scale investigations of the groundwater resources in all or part of the lower Chamokane Valley, the second includes multi-basin studies relating to the water resources of the entire Spokane Indian Reservation (Reservation), and the third includes basin-wide studies focused on the surface-water system of Chamokane Creek and its tributaries.

Detailed analysis of the upper aquifer within the Chamokane Valley is described by Buchanan and others (1988) and by Wozniewicz (1989). Numerous small-scale hydrogeologic and water-quality studies related to the closure of Dawn Mining Company's millsite are summarized by Washington Department of Health (1991). A geophysical seismic reflection survey was conducted to estimate the thickness of aquifer material near Ford by King and others (1996).

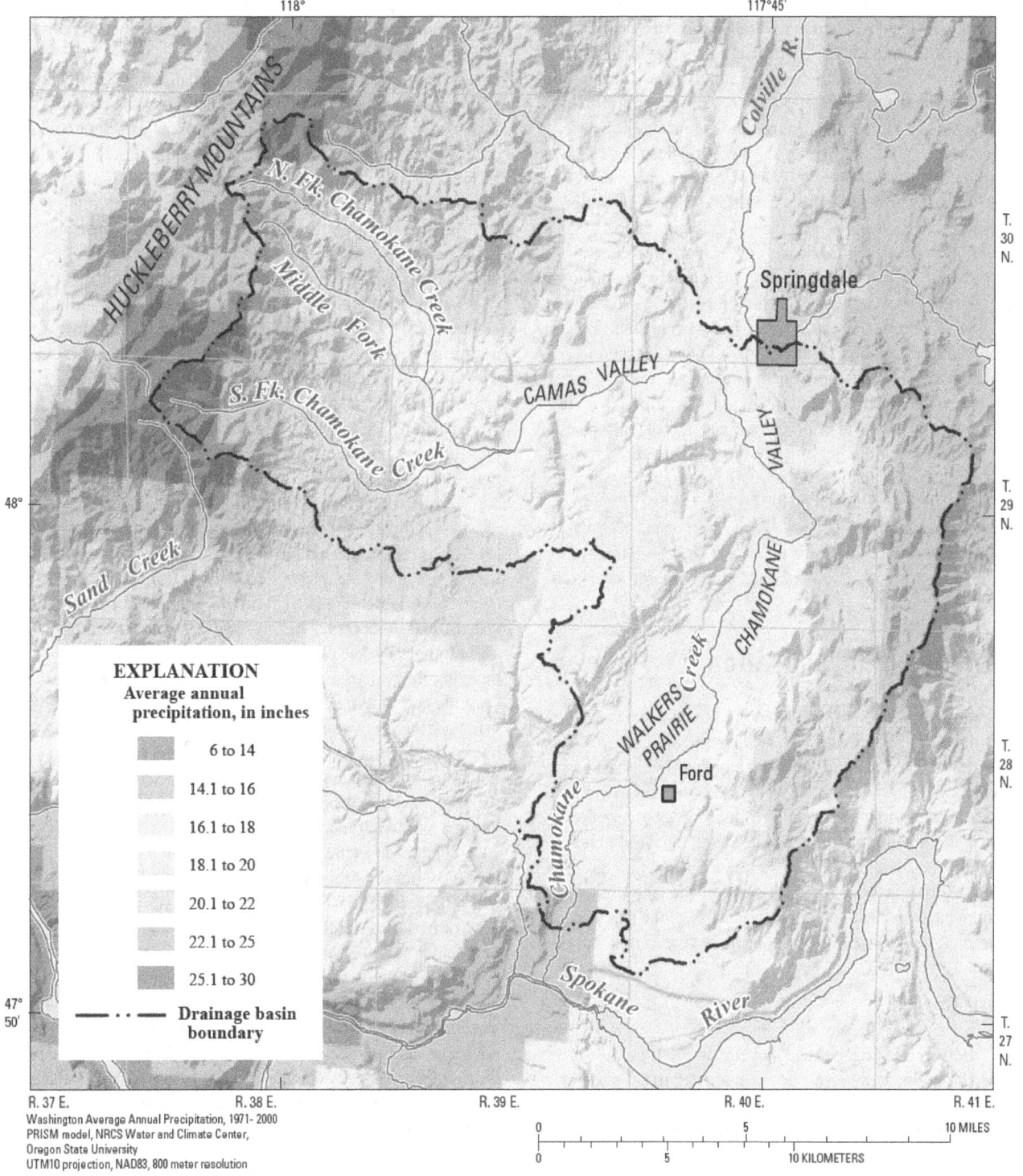

Figure 2. Average annual (1971–2000) precipitation in the Chamokane Creek basin study area, Stevens County, Washington.

Water resources of parts of the Spokane Indian Reservation are described in several documents. Lukas (1981) conducted a hydrogeologic study and described groundwater potential for domestic supply on the Reservation. Aquifer systems of the Reservation are described in Matt and Buchanan (1993a) and hydrology and geomorphology are described in Matt and Buchanan (1993b). These topics also are described in their entirety by Matt (1994). Peone and others (1993) produced an inventory of surface and groundwater resources on the Reservation including identification of factors that may affect water quality. Embry and others (1997) described the hydrogeologic units and groundwater quality of the eastern Reservation area including part of Walkers Prairie.

The Chamokane Creek Watershed Management Planning project addresses the improvement, maintenance, and protection of surface-water quality in the basin. The Watershed Management Plan (Kessler, 2000a) was developed to be used as a tool to guide local efforts to protect and (or) improve the surface-water quality on and off the Reservation. Kessler (2000b) reported surface-water quality and quantity measured in the basin from November 1997 through April 1999. In the *Chamokane Creek Watershed Needs Assessment*, Kessler (2008) described causes and sources of pollution, alternate management practices, and a water-quality monitoring plan.

Methods of Investigation

Collecting the basic data required to characterize the hydrogeologic framework and analyze the direction of groundwater movement in the Chamokane Creek basin involved a field inventory of wells, measurement of water levels in wells, and construction of hydrogeologic sections, hydrogeologic unit maps, and water-level maps. Methods used to collect and interpret these hydrogeologic data are presented in this section. Methods used to describe the land use and land change characterization and the water use of the study area are presented with those respective sections later in this report.

Well Data

Between September and November 2007, 102 wells throughout the study area were field located to acquire lithologic data and to measure the depth to water in wells. Criteria for site selection included availability of a driller's report and lithologic information (obtained from well records at the USGS Washington Water Science Center and the Washington Department of Ecology), location and depth of the well, and the ease of access to the well. The intent was to collect data from wells evenly distributed throughout the unconsolidated deposits of the study area, including the Camas and Chamokane Valley floors and tributary valleys.

This was not possible in all areas, however, because of lack of development in much of the basin or lack of permission to access some wells.

An additional 41 wells, field-located during previous USGS projects (Embrey and others, 1997; Kahle and others, 2003) were added to the Chamokane project data set to aid in describing the hydrogeologic framework of the study area. To further augment the project data set, 15 non-field-located wells were assigned approximate locations (latitude and longitude coordinates) using public land survey locations (township, range, section, and quarter-quarter section), well addresses, and (or) parcel number for each well included on drillers' logs. To the extent possible, paper maps (USGS 7 ½-minute quadrangles and City or County road maps) and on-line maps (Stevens County Assessor, 2010; National Geographic TOPO!, 2007; and Google™Earth, 2010) were used to verify drillers' locations and to estimate latitude and longitude for the 15 non-field-located wells. Locations of all 158 project wells are shown on plate 1, and selected physical and hydrologic data for the wells are provided in table 1.

Information gathered at field-located wells included site location and well-construction details. Depth to water (water level) was measured in most wells using a calibrated electric tape or graduated steel tape, both with accuracy to 0.01 ft. In some cases, water levels were not measured because a well was difficult to access. Two inventoried wells, 28N/39E-24K01 and 29N/39E-02J01, were observed as flowing, meaning the water level was above the land surface elevation. Latitude and longitude were obtained for field-located wells using a Global Positioning System (GPS) receiver with a horizontal accuracy of one-tenth of a second (about 10 ft). Land-surface altitude for each project well was obtained from a digital elevation model with 10-m square cells using the latitude and longitude for each well.

In addition to the water levels measured during the inventory phase of this study, synoptic water levels were measured in most of the field-inventoried wells during two 2-week periods, March 24–April 1, 2008, and August 25–September 4, 2008. Water levels also were measured monthly in a network of 25 wells during March 2008 through December 2009. Due to unusually heavy snow and inaccessibility of well heads, water-level measurements were not made in December 2008 and January 2009. Six wells in the monthly network also were instrumented with transducers for recording hourly water-level measurements from May 2008 through April 2010.

All water-level measurements were made by USGS personnel according to standardized techniques of the USGS (Drost, 2005). Information for all project wells was entered into the USGS National Water Information System (NWIS) database. Graphs of water-level altitude for selected wells are shown on plate 1.

Table 1. Selected physical and hydrologic data for the project wells in the Chamokane Creek basin, Stevens County, Washington.

[**Site No.**: See well- and spring-numbering system diagram for explanation of well- and spring-numbering system. **Depth of hole**: na, not applicable. **Land-surface altitude:** Referenced to the North American Vertical Datum of 1988 (NAVD 88). **Latitude and longitude:** In degrees, minutes, seconds referenced to the North American Datum of 1983 (NAD 83). **Location**: F, field located; N, not field located. **Hydrogeologic unit of open interval**: UA, Upper outwash aquifer; LU, Landslide unit; VC, Valley confining unit; LA, Lower aquifer; BT, Basalt unit; BR, Bedrock unit; other, unconsolidated deposits along the Spokane River. **Network**: M, manual monthly water-level measurements; T, transducer hourly water-level measurements; –, not part of network]

Site No.	Depth of hole (feet below land surface)	Land-surface altitude (feet)	Latitude	Longitude	Location	Hydrogeologic unit of open interval	Network
27N/39E-01E01	544	1,732	475216	1175021	N	BR	–
27N/39E-10L01	150	1,442	475106	1175245	F	other	–
27N/39E-11L01	361	1,549	475115	1175125	N	other	–
27N/39E-15A01	157	1,398	475045	1175156	N	other	–
27N/40E-18F01	340	1,742	475033	1174840	N	other	–
28N/39E-02Q01	278	2,424	475703	1175115	F	BT	–
28N/39E-02Q02	unknown	2,425	475702	1175114	F	BT	–
28N/39E-12R01	96	1,838	475610	1174939	F	LU	–
28N/39E-13B02	103	1,814	475552	1174945	F	LU	–
28N/39E-13B03	100	1,814	475555	1174941	F	LU	–
28N/39E-13C01	99	1,809	475547	1174960	F	LU	–
28N/39E-19R03	380	1,841	475416	1175559	F	BR	–
28N/39E-20P01	89	1,826	475420	1175523	F	LU	–
28N/39E-22Q01	100	1,822	475426	1175220	F	LU	–
28N/39E-22R02	565	1,784	475428	1175203	F	LU,BT	–
28N/39E-23E01	262	1,819	475446	1175154	F	LU,BT	–
28N/39E-23J01	160	1,683	475437	1175037	F	LA	M
28N/39E-23M01	218	1,804	475432	1175137	F	VC	M
28N/39E-23P01	247	1,691	475426	1175124	F	LA	–
28N/39E-23P02	255	1,697	475425	1175126	F	LA	–
28N/39E-24C02	326	1,790	475503	1175014	F	LA	–
28N/39E-24F01	358	1,762	475451	1174959	F	LA	–
28N/39E-24G03D1	280	1,746	475450	1174944	F	VC	–
28N/39E-24G04	380	1,727	475446	1174945	F	LA	–
28N/39E-24K01	256	1,685	475433	1174945	F	VC	–
28N/39E-24R01	75	1,764	475421	1174932	F	VC	–
28N/39E-26E01	350	1,759	475350	1175151	F	LA	M
28N/39E-26G01	115	1,619	475353	1175102	F	VC	–
28N/39E-27H01	359	1,760	475350	1175157	F	LA	–
28N/39E-27H02	220	1,760	475350	1175156	F	LA	–
28N/39E-27H03	385	1,761	475351	1175157	F	LA	–
28N/39E-27J01	327	1,749	475338	1175158	F	LA	–
28N/39E-27Q01	220	1,744	475324	1175216	F	LA	–
28N/39E-28A01	340	1,857	475405	1175326	F	VC,BR	–
28N/39E-28D01	320	1,837	475409	1175429	F	VC	–
28N/39E-29D01	178	1,831	475410	1175543	F	BR	–
28N/39E-34A01	280	1,744	475322	1175159	F	LA	–
28N/39E-34B01	187	1,734	475320	1175219	F	LA	–
28N/39E-34B02	180	1,736	475322	1175222	F	LA	–
28N/39E-35L01	131	1,719	475257	1175119	F	LA	–
28N/39E-35R01	400	1,721	475240	1175046	N	BR	–

Table 1.   Selected physical and hydrologic data for the project wells in the Chamokane Creek basin, Stevens County, Washington.—Continued

[**Site No.**: See well- and spring-numbering system diagram for explanation of well- and spring-numbering system. **Depth of hole**: na, not applicable. **Land-surface altitude:** Referenced to the North American Vertical Datum of 1988 (NAVD 88). **Latitude and longitude:** In degrees, minutes, seconds referenced to the North American Datum of 1983 (NAD 83). **Location**: F, field located; N, not field located. **Hydrogeologic unit of open interval**: UA, Upper outwash aquifer; LU, Landslide unit; VC, Valley confining unit; LA, Lower aquifer; BT, Basalt unit; BR, Bedrock unit; other, unconsolidated deposits along the Spokane River. **Network**: M, manual monthly water-level measurements; T, transducer hourly water-level measurements; –, not part of network]

Site No.	Depth of hole (feet below land surface)	Land-surface altitude (feet)	Latitude	Longitude	Location	Hydrogeologic unit of open interval	Network
28N/39E-36D01	303	1,855	475313	1175017	N	BR	–
28N/39E-36D02	302	1,852	475317	1175022	N	BT	–
28N/40E-03M01	60	1,855	475708	1174517	F	UA	M
28N/40E-05A01	80	1,834	475737	1174703	F	UA	M
28N/40E-05A02	261	1,833	475741	1174647	F	LA	M
28N/40E-05A03	320	1,833	475741	1174647	F	BR	–
28N/40E-05H01	40	1,833	475730	1174656	F	UA	–
28N/40E-05Q01	60	1,836	475657	1174713	F	UA	–
28N/40E-06R01	283	1,864	475656	1174811	F	LA	M
28N/40E-07N02	115	1,815	475602	1174919	F	UA	–
28N/40E-08H02	43	1,820	475629	1174649	F	UA	T
28N/40E-08K01	80	1,824	475624	1174704	F	UA	–
28N/40E-09A01	89	1,865	475648	1174532	F	UA	–
28N/40E-09A02	140	1,835	475646	1174540	F	BR	–
28N/40E-11H02	120	2,118	475636	1174304	F	BR	M
28N/40E-17C01	380	1,817	475558	1174734	F	LA	T
28N/40E-17F01	121	1,810	475539	1174723	F	LA	–
28N/40E-17F02	155	1,810	475539	1174724	F	LA	–
28N/40E-17J01	20	1,793	475525	1174655	F	UA	T
28N/40E-17K01	47	1,793	475532	1174719	F	UA	T
28N/40E-17L01	41	1,807	475533	1174727	F	UA	–
28N/40E-18Q01	440	1,796	475514	1174838	F	LA	–
28N/40E-18Q02	58	1,777	475510	1174840	F	UA	–
28N/40E-18Q03	58	1,787	475512	1174837	F	UA	–
28N/40E-18Q04	22	1,776	475510	1174840	F	UA	T
28N/40E-19D01	42	1,774	475508	1174906	F	UA	–
28N/40E-19E01S	na	1,725	475444	1174920	F	UA	–
28N/40E-19J02	158	1,779	475437	1174819	F	BT	–
28N/40E-30D01	367	1,767	475406	1174914	F	LA	M
28N/40E-30D02	120	1,775	475415	1174900	F	BR	–
28N/40E-30D03	200	1,766	475408	1174912	F	LA	–
28N/40E-31D01	264	1,874	475316	1174914	F	VC	–
29N/38E-02R01R1	100	2,536	480205	1175817	F	BR	–
29N/38E-11A01	120	2,531	480153	1175819	F	BR	–
29N/38E-36M01	100	2,504	475804	1175825	F	BT	–
29N/39E-01C01	52	2,156	480254	1175019	F	UA,VC	–
29N/39E-02J01	258	2,151	480223	1175058	F	LA	–
29N/39E-02R01	14	2,156	480209	1175056	F	UA	M
29N/39E-03J01	40	2,185	480230	1175203	F	BT	–
29N/39E-03J02	210	2,177	480227	1175203	F	BR	–

Table 1. Selected physical and hydrologic data for the project wells in the Chamokane Creek basin, Stevens County, Washington.—Continued

[**Site No.**: See well- and spring-numbering system diagram for explanation of well- and spring-numbering system. **Depth of hole**: na, not applicable. **Land-surface altitude:** Referenced to the North American Vertical Datum of 1988 (NAVD 88). **Latitude and longitude:** In degrees, minutes, seconds referenced to the North American Datum of 1983 (NAD 83). **Location**: F, field located; N, not field located. **Hydrogeologic unit of open interval**: UA, Upper outwash aquifer; LU, Landslide unit; VC, Valley confining unit; LA, Lower aquifer; BT, Basalt unit; BR, Bedrock unit; other, unconsolidated deposits along the Spokane River. **Network**: M, manual monthly water-level measurements; T, transducer hourly water-level measurements; –, not part of network]

Site No.	Depth of hole (feet below land surface)	Land-surface altitude (feet)	Latitude	Longitude	Location	Hydrogeologic unit of open interval	Network
29N/39E-10G01	100	2,177	480145	1175226	F	BR	–
29N/39E-16F01	200	2,184	480058	1175356	F	VC	M
29N/40E-03C02	242	2,090	480252	1174450	F	VC	–
29N/40E-04C01	300	2,170	480255	1174623	N	BT	–
29N/40E-04K02	138	2,044	480219	1174554	F	UA	–
29N/40E-04K03	100	2,034	480227	1174555	F	UA	–
29N/40E-05A02	108	2,147	480254	1174653	F	BT	–
29N/40E-05P01	500	2,526	480207	1174730	F	BT,BR	–
29N/40E-05P02	500	2,544	480209	1174727	F	BT	–
29N/40E-06C01	324	2,137	480254	1174904	N	UA	–
29N/40E-06D01	358	2,143	480254	1174920	F	LA	M
29N/40E-09G01	65	1,971	480150	1174554	F	UA	–
29N/40E-09G02	336	1,971	480138	1174548	F	LA	–
29N/40E-09G03	73	1,968	480143	1174552	F	UA	M
29N/40E-09G04	165	1,970	480148	1174553	F	VC	–
29N/40E-09L01	400	2,008	480125	1174609	N	BR	–
29N/40E-10D01	100	1,993	480154	1174508	F	UA	–
29N/40E-10F01R1	240	1,974	480143	1174458	F	UA	–
29N/40E-10K01	41	1,958	480136	1174445	F	UA	–
29N/40E-10L01	58	1,952	480136	1174455	F	UA	–
29N/40E-12E01	147	2,035	480147	1174251	F	BR	–
29N/40E-14D01	280	2,006	480101	1174356	F	UA	–
29N/40E-15J02	60	1,915	480035	1174423	F	UA	–
29N/40E-15J03	105	1,912	480035	1174425	F	UA	–
29N/40E-15K02	340	1,927	480036	1174442	N	UA	–
29N/40E-15Q02	460	1,942	480019	1174429	F	LA	M
29N/40E-15R02	120	1,899	480028	1174416	F	UA	M
29N/40E-22E01	163	1,934	480004	1174514	F	BT	–
29N/40E-22J02	60	1,878	475943	1174427	F	UA	M
29N/40E-22P01	110	1,867	475937	1174502	F	LU	M
29N/40E-22Q01	61	1,868	475937	1174445	F	UA	–
29N/40E-23C01	69	1,886	480012	1174335	F	UA	–
29N/40E-23M02	96	1,891	475950	1174407	F	UA	–
29N/40E-23M03	80	1,888	475948	1174407	F	UA	–
29N/40E-23M04	80	1,888	475949	1174411	F	UA	–
29N/40E-23M05	140	1,888	475948	1174407	F	UA	–
29N/40E-23M06	80	1,885	475944	1174351	F	UA	M
29N/40E-26C02	225	1,948	475914	1174346	F	BR	–

Table 1.   Selected physical and hydrologic data for the project wells in the Chamokane Creek basin, Stevens County, Washington.—Continued

[Site No.: See well- and spring-numbering system diagram for explanation of well- and spring-numbering system. **Depth of hole**: na, not applicable. **Land-surface altitude:** Referenced to the North American Vertical Datum of 1988 (NAVD 88). **Latitude and longitude:** In degrees, minutes, seconds referenced to the North American Datum of 1983 (NAD 83). **Location**: F, field located; N, not field located. **Hydrogeologic unit of open interval**: UA, Upper outwash aquifer; LU, Landslide unit; VC, Valley confining unit; LA, Lower aquifer; BT, Basalt unit; BR, Bedrock unit; other, unconsolidated deposits along the Spokane River. **Network**: M, manual monthly water-level measurements; T, transducer hourly water-level measurements; –, not part of network]

Site No.	Depth of hole (feet below land surface)	Land-surface altitude (feet)	Latitude	Longitude	Location	Hydrogeologic unit of open interval	Network
29N/40E-26C03	150	1,982	475914	1174330	F	UA	–
29N/40E-26D01	160	1,957	475915	1174405	F	UA	–
29N/40E-26D02	215	1,955	475918	1174356	F	UA	–
29N/40E-26E01	150	1,944	475901	1174355	F	UA	–
29N/40E-28J01	60	1,854	475858	1174536	F	LU	–
29N/40E-28P01	48	1,855	475836	1174607	N	UA	T
29N/40E-33C01	80	1,851	475824	1174612	F	UA	–
29N/40E-33E01	55	1,895	475822	1174637	F	LU	–
29N/40E-33M01	149	1,845	475760	1174634	F	VC	–
29N/40E-33M02	53	1,845	475760	1174634	F	UA	–
29N/40E-33M03	50	1,844	475758	1174634	F	UA	–
29N/40E-34F02	100	1,893	475812	1174450	F	UA	–
29N/40E-34H02	140	1,924	475818	1174418	F	UA	–
29N/40E-34H03	140	1,924	475815	1174421	F	UA	–
29N/40E-34J01	100	1,915	475807	1174425	F	UA	–
30N/39E-25Q02	107	2,213	480358	1174946	F	UA	M
30N/39E-25Q03	200	2,210	480358	1174955	F	BT	–
30N/39E-29A01	325	2,737	480423	1175430	F	BR	–
30N/39E-30B01	380	2,487	480430	1175615	F	BT	–
30N/39E-36L02	500	2,168	480315	1175007	N	VC	–
30N/40E-21H01	240.5	1,901	480514	1174533	F	LA	–
30N/40E-28A01D1	240	1,947	480433	1174541	F	LA	–
30N/40E-30K01D1	520	2,367	480410	1174839	N	BR	–
30N/40E-31M01	60	2,145	480314	1174911	F	VC	–
30N/40E-31N01	120	2,142	480301	1174915	F	VC	–
30N/40E-31P01D1	289	2,197	480309	1174859	N	BT	–
30N/40E-31Q04	340	2,135	480302	1174811	F	BT	–
30N/40E-32C01D1	170	2,141	480336	1174733	F	BT	–
30N/40E-32F01	140	2,183	480326	1174734	F	BT	–
30N/40E-32F03	121	2,145	480335	1174733	F	BT	–
30N/40E-32G02	62	2,107	480334	1174719	F	UA	–
30N/40E-32L01	70	2,210	480319	1174732	F	BT	–
30N/40E-32P01	75	2,124	480302	1174744	F	UA	–
30N/40E-33L01	154	2,064	480320	1174615	F	UA	–
30N/40E-33M01	80	2,077	480312	1174633	F	UA	–
30N/40E-33N01	360	2,138	480309	1174627	F	BR	–
30N/40E-33R01R1	190	2,026	480302	1174537	F	VC	–
30N/40E-33R02	340	1,990	480257	1174534	F	VC	–
30N/40E-33R03	46	1,982	480306	1174533	F	UA	–

Geology

The geologic map of the study area (pl. 2) was compiled and simplified from several sources, including previously unpublished surficial geologic mapping of the Ford and Tum Tum, Washington 7 ½-minute quadrangles (Dr. Eugene Kiver, Eastern Washington University Emeritus, written commun., October 2007), the surficial geologic map of the Chewelah 1:100,000 quadrangle (Carrara and others, 1995), the digital geologic map database (1:100,000 scale) for Washington (Washington Division of Geology and Earth Resources, 2005), and detailed streambed mapping between Ford and Chamokane Falls (Howard and others, 1989 and Howard, 1990). In some areas, modifications were made to existing maps based on field visits or stratigraphic evidence obtained during this investigation, primarily from drillers' logs for field-located water wells.

Hydrogeology

Lithologic data from the field-inventoried wells were entered into the Rockworks 2006® software, a stratigraphic analysis package. Sixteen hydrogeologic sections were constructed using Rockworks to identify and correlate hydrogeologic units, primarily on the basis of grain size and stratigraphic position. To avoid redundancy, nine representative sections of the original 16 are published in this report. Thickness and extent-of-unit maps were manually drawn for two units using information from the hydrogeologic sections and data from the remaining project wells.

The altitude of the top and extent of hydrogeologic units described in this report were used to create digital elevation model (DEM) surfaces with 30 ft square cells in a Geographic Information System (GIS) database. These surfaces provide the digital framework for the GSFLOW model being developed for Phase 2 of this project. The interpolation method for creating each hydrogeologic unit surface in GIS was based on the Australian National University Digital Elevation Model (ANUDEM) procedure developed by Hutchinson (1989), using top-of-unit altitudes at wells and extent maps. Each hydrogeologic unit surface was constrained to the National Elevation Dataset (NED) 30 ft DEM for land surface where the unit outcropped.

In developing the digital hydrogeologic framework, the original data interpretations were honored as much as possible. The interpolated hydrogeologic unit surfaces and thicknesses were compared to the original hydrogeologic unit maps, hydrogeologic sections, and well interpretations in order to make adjustments that more accurately reflect the original interpretations. Uncertainties are greatest in areas where the surficial geology changes abruptly or gaps exist in the lithologic data provided by the project wells.

Meteorological Data

Data from an automated agricultural weather station (AgriMet station) installed and operated by the Bureau of Reclamation (http://www.usbr.gov/pn/agrimet/) was used to estimate evapotranspiration (ET) in the Chamokane Creek basin. The AgriMet station was installed in the north-central part of the study area in November 2007 and will be operated continuously through December 2010. AgriMet uses the 1982 Kimberly-Penman equation, adapted by the U.S. Department of Agriculture (USDA) Agricultural Research Service (Jensen and others, 1990), for computing reference ET. This procedure requires several meteorological input parameters for modeling ET, including maximum and minimum daily air temperatures, relative humidity, daily solar radiation, and daily wind run, all of which are collected by the AgriMet system (Peter Palmer, Bureau of Reclamation, written commun., September 12, 2006). Data collected by this station are available on-line at http://www.usbr.gov/pn/agrimet/agrimetmap/chawda.html.

Geology and Geologic Setting

Chamokane Creek basin is in the eastern part of the Okanogan Highlands, a physiographic region east of the Columbia River and Franklin D. Roosevelt Lake and north of the Columbia Plateau (fig. 3). This area is characterized by north-south trending mountain ranges reaching altitudes of 8,000 ft separated by valleys including the Colville River and Chamokane Creek Valleys. The Okanogan Highlands contain the oldest sedimentary and metamorphic rocks in Washington State (Lasmanis, 1991; table 2). Precambrian metasedimentary rocks including argillite, dolomite, gneiss, schist, slate, and quartzite extend from British Columbia south to near the Spokane River (Stoffel and others, 1991). Precambrian metasedimentary rocks are overlain by younger marine sedimentary rocks that represent each of the geologic-time periods in the Paleozoic Era (table 2) and include quartzite, shale, and limestone (Lasmanis, 1991). Cretaceous Period and Eocene Epoch granites that intruded the older rocks are exposed at land surface throughout the Okanogan Highlands including much of the western part of the Spokane Indian Reservation.

During the Miocene Epoch, basalt flows spread northeast from the Columbia Plateau mantling much of the pre-existing landscape and filling in low-lying areas, including part of the area within the Chamokane Creek basin. A basalt capped mesa is located on the eastern part of the Spokane Indian Reservation extending from near Wellpinit to Lyons Hill and forms the western edge of Walkers Prairie (pl. 2).

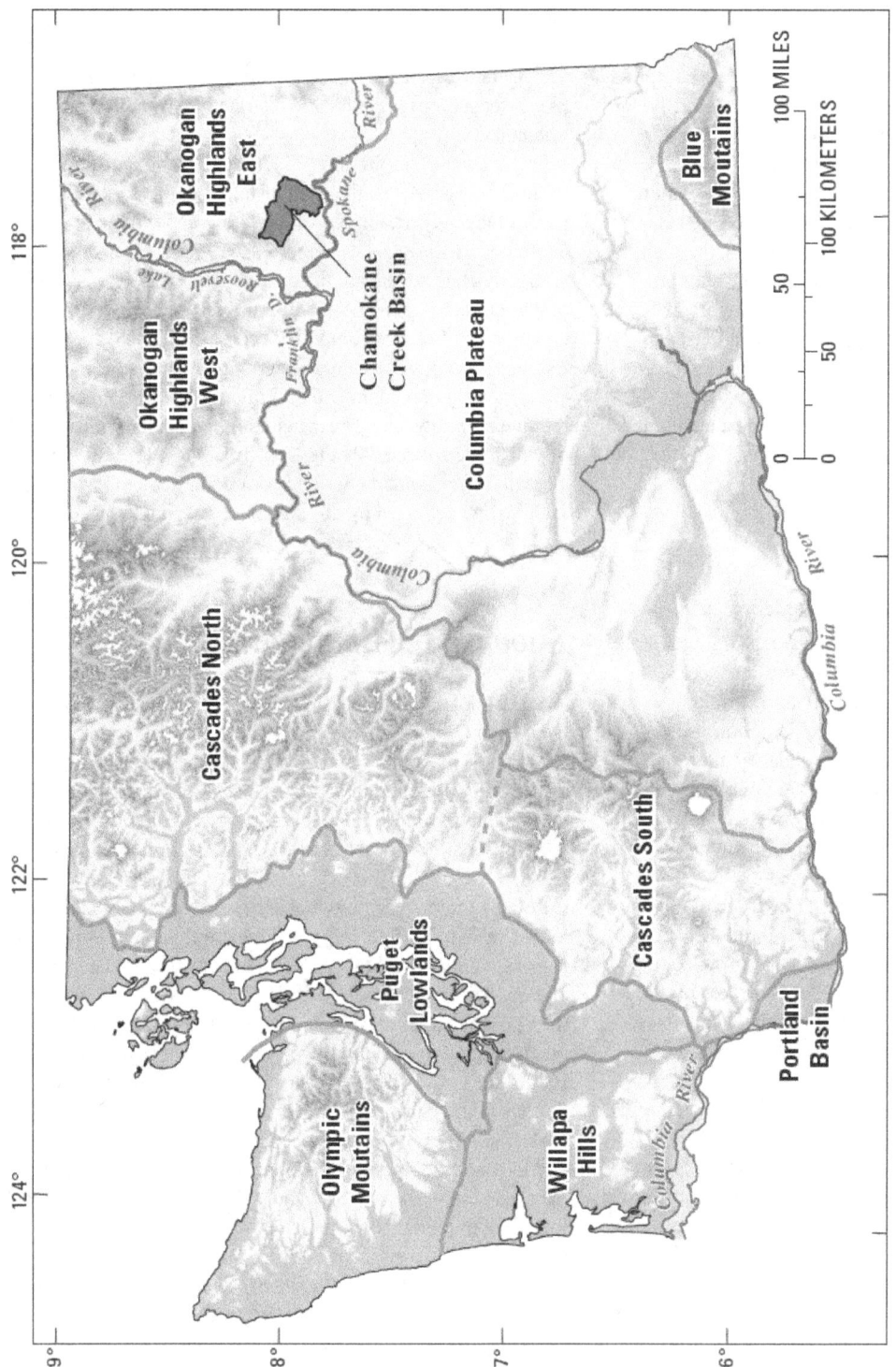

Figure 3.   Physiographic regions of Washington. (Modified from Lasmanis, 1991.)

Table 2. Geologic timescale with simplified geologic units of the Chamokane Creek basin study area, Stevens County, Washington.

[Modified from Kahle and Bartolino, 2007. **Abbreviations**: ya, years ago; mya, million years ago; –, indicates a gap in the geologic record resulting from erosion and (or) nondeposition]

Geologic Time				Simplified geologic unit
Phanerozoic Eon (544 mya to present)	Cenozoic Era (65 mya to present)	Quaternary Period (1.8 mya to present)	Holocene Epoch (8,000 ya to present)	Recent non-glacial sediment
			Pleistocene Epoch (1.8 mya to 8,000 ya)	Glacial deposits and catastrophic flood deposits
		Tertiary Period (65 to 1.8 mya)	Pliocene Epoch (5.3 to 1.8 mya)	–
			Miocene Epoch (23.8 to 5.3 mya)	Basalt and older sediments
			Oligocene Epoch (33.7 to 23.8 mya)	–
			Eocene Epoch (55.5 to 33.7 mya)	Intrusive igneous rocks (granite)
			Paleocene Epoch (65 to 55.5 mya)	
	Mesozoic Era (248 to 65 mya)	Cretaceous Period (145 to 65 mya)		
		Jurassic Period (213 to 145 mya)		–
		Triassic Period (248 to 213 mya)		
	Paleozoic Era (544 to 248 mya)	Permian Period (286 to 248 mya)		Marine sedimentary rocks
		Carboniferous Period (360 to 286 mya)		
		Devonian Period (410 to 360 mya)		
		Silurian Period (440 to 410 mya)		
		Ordovician Period (505 to 440 mya)		
		Cambrian Period (544 to 505 mya)		
Precambrian Time (4,500 to 544 mya)	Proterozoic (2,500 to 544 mya)			Metasedimentary rocks
	Archean (3,800 to 2,500 mya)			–
	Hadean (4,500 to 3,800 mya)			

During the Pleistocene Epoch, the study area was subjected repeatedly to the erosional and depositional processes associated with glacial and interglacial periods (Kiver and Stradling, 1982 and Kiver and others, 1989). This resulted in an assemblage of unconsolidated sediment that overlies much of the bedrock in the study area and is thickest along the valley floors.

At the maximum extent of the most recent Pleistocene glaciation (about 15,000 years before present), much of northern Washington, Idaho, and westernmost Montana was covered by lobes of the Cordilleran ice sheet (fig. 4). The large ice sheet formed in the mountains of British Columbia and flowed south, filling valleys and overriding low mountain ranges in the northern parts of Washington, Idaho, and Montana. For thousands of years, the Okanogan, Columbia River, and Purcell Trench lobes of the Cordilleran ice sheet covered much of northeastern Washington and northern Idaho. The Okanogan lobe to the west of the combined Colville-Chamokane Valley was the largest of the lobes and covered what is now the northern part of the Waterville Plateau. The Okanogan and Columbia River lobes affected the study area by blocking westward drainage of the ancestral Columbia and Spokane Rivers and creating vast ice-age lakes (Waitt and Thorson, 1983). A sublobe of the Columbia River lobe moved into the Colville Valley and reached its southernmost extent near Springdale, Wash.. Ice thickness in the Colville Valley was at least 2,300 ft (Carrara and others, 1995).

When the Purcell Trench lobe in northern Idaho blocked the drainage of the ancestral Clark Fork in northwestern Montana, Glacial Lake Missoula was created (fig. 4). Although much of the unconsolidated deposits in the study area are the result of glacial processes involving the Okanogan and Columbia lobes and the Colville sublobe, the Purcell Trench lobe, in what is now northern Idaho, also contributed directly to sedimentation in the Chamokane Creek basin. Glacial Lake Missoula, dammed behind the Purcell Trench lobe (fig. 4), was about 600 mi^3 in volume and reached a maximum depth of 2,200 ft (Waitt, 1980). Enormous catastrophic floods occurred over a 2,000-year period when the ice dam of the Purcell Trench lobe periodically failed, sending floodwaters west and southwest. Floodwater crossed parts of Montana, Idaho, Washington, and Oregon before reaching the Pacific Ocean (fig. 4). The continuous southward flow of ice repeatedly blocked the Clark Fork allowing Lake Missoula to refill multiple times. The largest of the Missoula floods, many of which probably occurred relatively early in the lake-filling and flooding cycle, overwhelmed local drainages and topped the 2,400-ft divide west of Spokane, spilling south towards Cheney and beyond and creating the Channeled Scablands (fig. 4). Some of the Missoula floods, following one of the more northern floodways, left behind giant current dunes north of Loon Lake before exiting westward through the Sheep Creek spillway into the Colville Valley near Springdale and then southward through the Chamokane Valley (pl. 2; Carrara and others, 1995).

Glacial Lake Columbia, impounded by the Okanogan lobe, was the largest glacial lake in the path of the Missoula floods (fig. 4). This lake was long-lived (2,000–3,000 years) and had a typical surface altitude of 1,640 ft; however, the altitude reached 2,350 ft during maximum blockage by the Okanogan lobe and rose as high as 2,460 ft during the Missoula floods (Atwater, 1986). The higher level of Glacial Lake Columbia probably occurred early, whereas the lower and more typical level of the lake occurred in later glacial time (Richmond and others, 1965; Waitt and Thorson, 1983; and Atwater, 1986). At the lower level (1,640 ft), Glacial Lake Columbia extended into the Chamokane Valley to near Ford and east to the Spokane area, where clayey lake sediment is intercalated with Missoula flood sediment. At the higher level of Glacial Lake Columbia (2,350 ft), the glacial lake would have flooded the entire combined Colville-Chamokane Valley nearly reaching the top of the basalt bluffs on the western edge of Walkers Prairie (pl. 2).

As the Colville sublobe advanced southward through the Colville Valley, till was deposited beneath the ice and fine-grained sediments were deposited as the lobe advanced into glacial Lake Columbia (Waitt and Thorson, 1983). The southernmost limit of the Colville sublobe is marked by a well-developed moraine near the town of Springdale (Carrara and others, 1996), where hummocky topography resulted from the deposition of material pushed along the ice front and from melting of sediment laden ice. This well-developed terminal moraine (pl. 2) is referred to as the Springdale moraine (Flint, 1936; Carrara and others, 1996). The outflow of glacial meltwater draining Camas Valley was pushed southward presumably by the front of the ice sublobe and the morainal material causing it to incise a narrow channel, Ice Box Canyon, (pl. 1) through a northern limb of Lyons Hill (McLucas, 1980).

Along the margins of the sublobe, glacial meltwater deposited large areas of outwash sands and gravels. Melt water from the Colville sublobe created a large outwash plain and series of gravel terraces extending from near Springdale to south of Ford. This meltwater deposited vast quantities of sediment and reworked early Lake Missoula flood deposits. Just beyond the southern limit of the sublobe are former glacial meltwater channels now occupied by Swamp Creek (fig. 1; pls. 1 and 2). Melt water from the diverted Deer Creek drainage contributed to the deposition of a terrace on the north wall of Camas Valley including the foot of Craney Hill (pl. 2; McLucas, 1980). These coarse-grained deposits overlie fine-grained sediment (clay and silt) that are presumed to be associated with Glacial Lake Columbia.

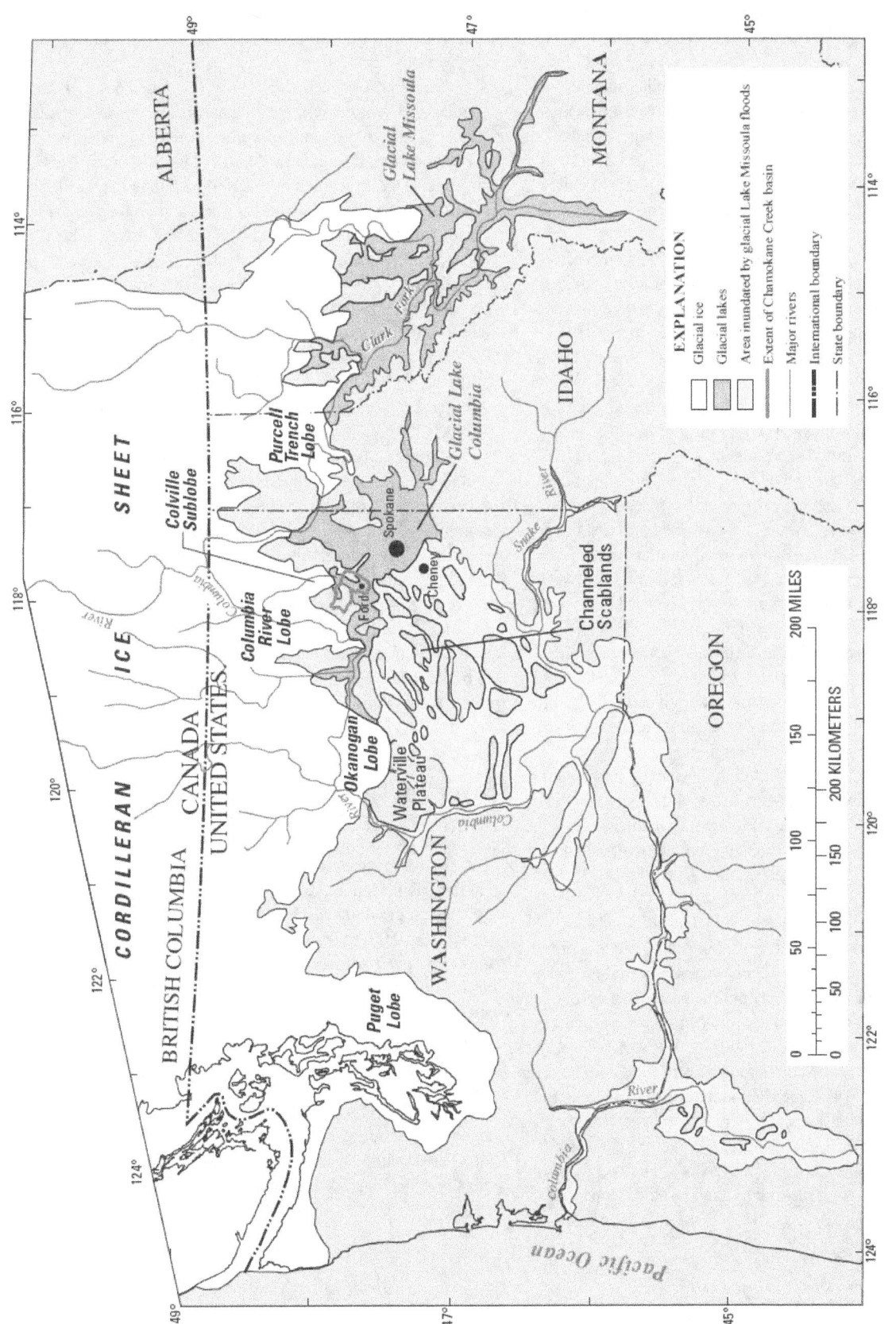

Figure 4. Extent of glacial ice and glacial lakes in northern Washington, Idaho, and parts of Montana. (Modified from Allen and Burns, 1986, and Atwater, 1986.)

The surficial geology of the study area consists of 10 geologic units that are described below and shown on plate 2.

Alluvial deposits (Qal): This unit includes channel and overbank deposits of Chamokane and Swamp Creeks and alluvial-fan deposits at the mouths of streams tributary to Chamokane Creek. The unit consists mostly of stratified silt and sand with some gravel and minor amounts of clay deposited by flowing water and generally is from 1 to 30 ft thick.

Glacial outburst flood deposits (Qf): This unit includes glacial-outburst flood deposits that consist of sand with sparse pebbles, cobbles, and boulders deposited by catastrophic draining of Glacial Lake Missoula into lower energy environments along the margins of the floods. These deposits are mapped in the southern part of basin. This unit is as much as 100 ft thick within the Chamokane Creek basin.

Glaciofluvial deposits (Qgf): This unit includes mostly stratified and well-sorted sand, gravel, and cobble outwash deposited by glacial meltwater from the Colville sublobe. It also includes outwash deposits along the northern part of the Camas Valley and outwash and reworked outburst flood deposits along the Chamokane Valley floor and Walkers Prairie. Although most of the Qgf is coarse-grained outwash, lenses of silt, clay, and till occur locally. The thickness of the unit generally is from 20 to 200 ft.

Glacial deposits, undifferentiated (Qgu): This unit includes a heterogeneous mixture of silt, sand, gravel, and clay that may include loess deposits and older glacial till. The unit mantles the upland areas in the west central part of the study area and generally is from 5 to 20 ft thick.

Glacial till (Qti): This unit includes mostly unsorted and unstratified clay, silt, sand, and gravel deposited by the Colville sublobe. Near Springdale, the unit includes the terminal moraine of the Colville sublobe. Locally, the unit contains stratified sand and gravel and generally, is from 10 to 80 ft thick.

Glaciolacustrine deposits (Qla): This unit includes mostly clay and silt lake sediments deposited in ice-marginal lakes. The unit underlies the Chamokane Creek Valley and is overlain by younger deposits within the basin. Just north of the Chamokane Creek basin, about 2 mi northeast of Springdale, the unit occurs at land surface in the Colville Valley floor. The unit includes thin and discontinuous beds of sand and gravel in places. Along the axis of the Chamokane Valley, the thickness of the unit is commonly about 300 ft.

Loess (Qlo): This unit includes silt and fine sand, and minor amounts of clay, deposited by winds. The unit forms an extensive blanket on the basalt upland of the Lyons Hill

area and has a limited extent to the east of Happy Hill in the southeast part of the study area. Thickness of the unit typically ranges from 1 to 15 ft.

Mass-wasting deposits (Qmw): Includes poorly sorted angular rock fragments deposited as talus at the base of steep slopes and heterogeneous mixtures of unconsolidated surficial material and rock fragments deposited by landslides. The largest surface exposures of this unit are along the basalt bluff on the western edge of Walkers Prairie and on the west side of Happy Hill near Ford. Thickness of the unit varies, but may exceed 200 ft in places.

Basalt (Miocene) (Mb): Includes the Grande Ronde Basalt of the Columbia River Basalt Group, a dense, dark basalt with fine to coarse interbeds. Interbeds may be part of the Latah Formation, which was deposited along the margins of the basalt flows in eastern Washington. Thickness of the unit in the study area is uncertain, but may be more than 500 ft.

Bedrock (Tertiary to Middle Proterozoic) (Tybr): Includes sedimentary, metasedimentary, and intrusive and extrusive igneous rocks. Specific rock types include shale, conglomerate, dolomite, limestone, argillite, gneiss, schist, slate, quartzite, and granite. The unit is exposed in much of the high-altitude areas of the basin. The depth to bedrock in the Chamokane Creek Valley beneath the unconsolidated sediments is largely unknown and likely varies considerably. Based on information from wells used in this study, the depth to bedrock along most of the central part of the Chamokane Creek Valley may be as much as 600 ft.

Hydrogeologic Framework

The geologic units described previously were grouped into six hydrogeologic units based on similar lithologic characteristics and large-scale hydrologic properties. The six hydrogeologic units described in this report include the Upper outwash aquifer, the Landslide unit, the Valley confining unit, the Lower aquifer, the Basalt unit, and the Bedrock unit. Lithologic and hydrologic characteristics of these units are summarized in figure 5. The surficial extent of the units is shown in figure 6 and the subsurface extent of the units is shown on the hydrogeologic sections (pl. 2) and in figures 7 and 8, for the Upper outwash aquifer and Valley confining unit, respectively. Project well locations are shown on plate 1 and are color coded based on the hydrogeologic unit that the wells are open to. Wells that are open to more than one unit are shown as black dots on plate 1.

Hydrogeologic unit	Unit label	Range of thickness [estimated average thickness] (feet)	Lithologic and hydrologic characteristics	Number of project wells open to unit
Upper outwash aquifer	UA	2–280 [80]	Unconfined aquifer consisting of gravel, cobbles, boulders, and sand with minor silt and or clay interbeds. Unit occurs in the Chamokane Valley from Swamp Creek southward throughout Walkers Prairie. UA occurs in Camas Valley, but is thinner and less productive. Includes geologic units Qgf, Qf, and Qal. Near Springdale, UA includes till (Qti), a lower-permeability deposit that includes compacted and poorly-sorted silt, sand, gravel, and cobbles with lenses of moderately sorted sand and gravel.	57
Landslide unit	LU	0–205 [150]	Poorly sorted deposits of broken basalt and sedimentary interbeds of the Columbia River Basalt Group, covered in places by glacial deposits. Unit occurs along the eastern slopes of the basalt mesa on the eastern uplands of the Spokane Indian Reservation and on the western flanks of Happy Hill near Ford. Unit likely is in hydraulic connnection with the UA in Walker's Prairie. Locally an aquifer with variable yields. Includes geologic unit Qmw.	9
Valley confining unit	VC	4–480 [170]	Low-permeability unit consisting mostly of glaciolacustrine silt and clay. Unit occurs at depth throughout the Camas and Chamokane Valleys and is continuous northward into the Colville Valley. Discontinuous lenses of aquifer material within the unit contributes usable quantities of water to some wells, particularly in the southern part of the basin where Missoula flood deposits are interbedded with the glaciolacustrine deposits.	16
Lower aquifer	LA	3–170	Confined aquifer consisting of sand and some gravel. Unit occurs at depth in the Camas and Chamokane Valleys below the Valley confining unit and is continuous northward into the Colville Valley. Thickness of unit is not well known.	30
Basalt unit	BT	40–500	Unit is composed of Columbia River Basalt, a dense, dark basalt with generally fine grained interbeds. Coarse-grained interbeds occur near Springdale. Water is contained in cracks and fractures and from zones between lava flows. Occurs in the eastern uplands of the Spokane Indian Reservation and on Lyons Hill. Includes geologic unit Mb and thin and discontinuous Qlo and Qgu.	18
Bedrock unit	BR	Not applicable	Unit includes argillite, conglomerate, dolomite, gneiss, schist, slate, quartzite, shale, limestone, and granite. Yields are generally small; numerous abandoned wells. Includes geologic unit Tybr and thin and discontinuous Qal, Qlo, and Qgf.	19

Figure 5.   Lithologic and hydrologic characteristics of the hydrogeologic units in the Chamokane Creek basin, Stevens County, Washington.

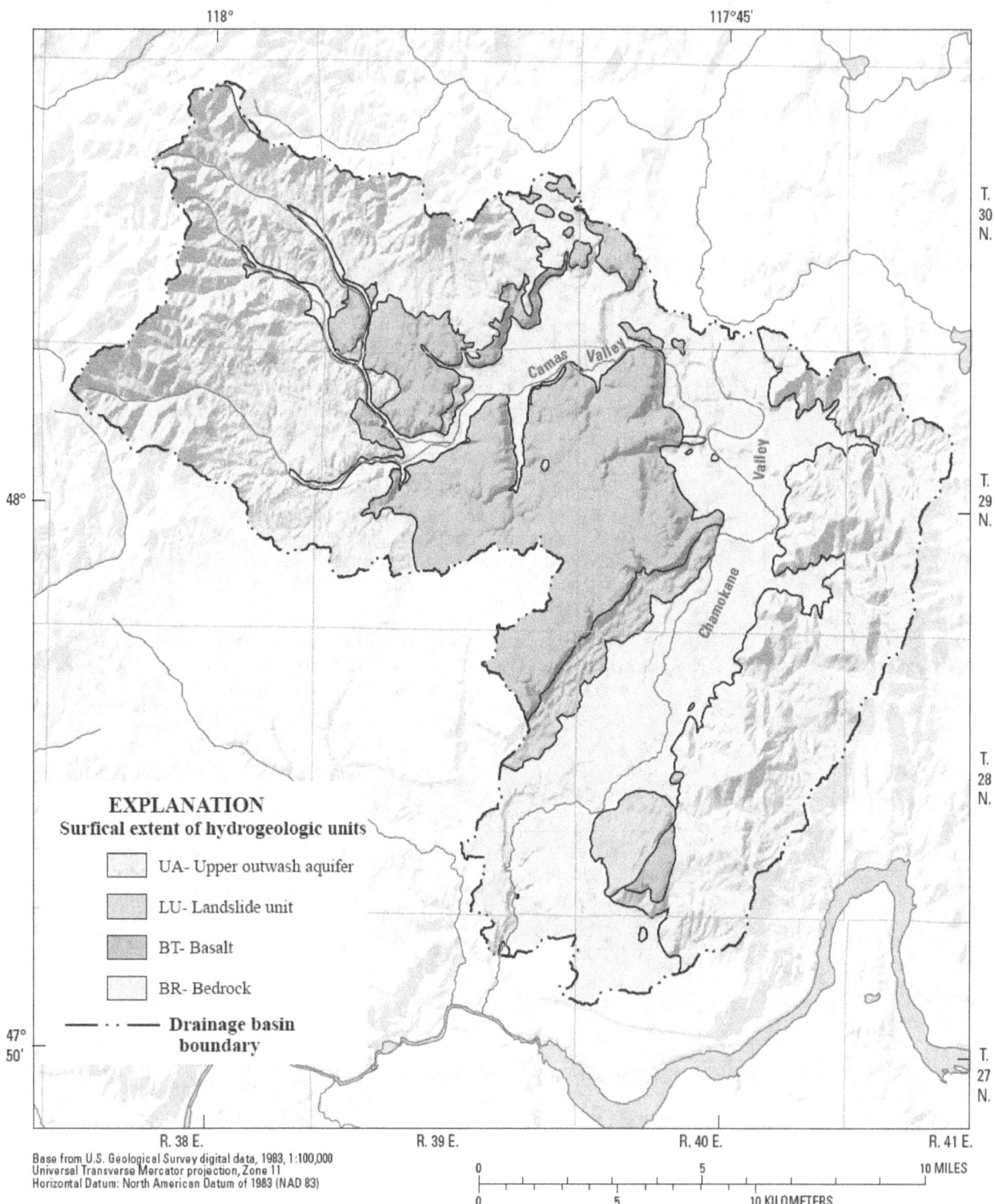

Figure 6. Surficial extent of the hydrogeologic units in the Chamokane Creek basin, Stevens County, Washington.

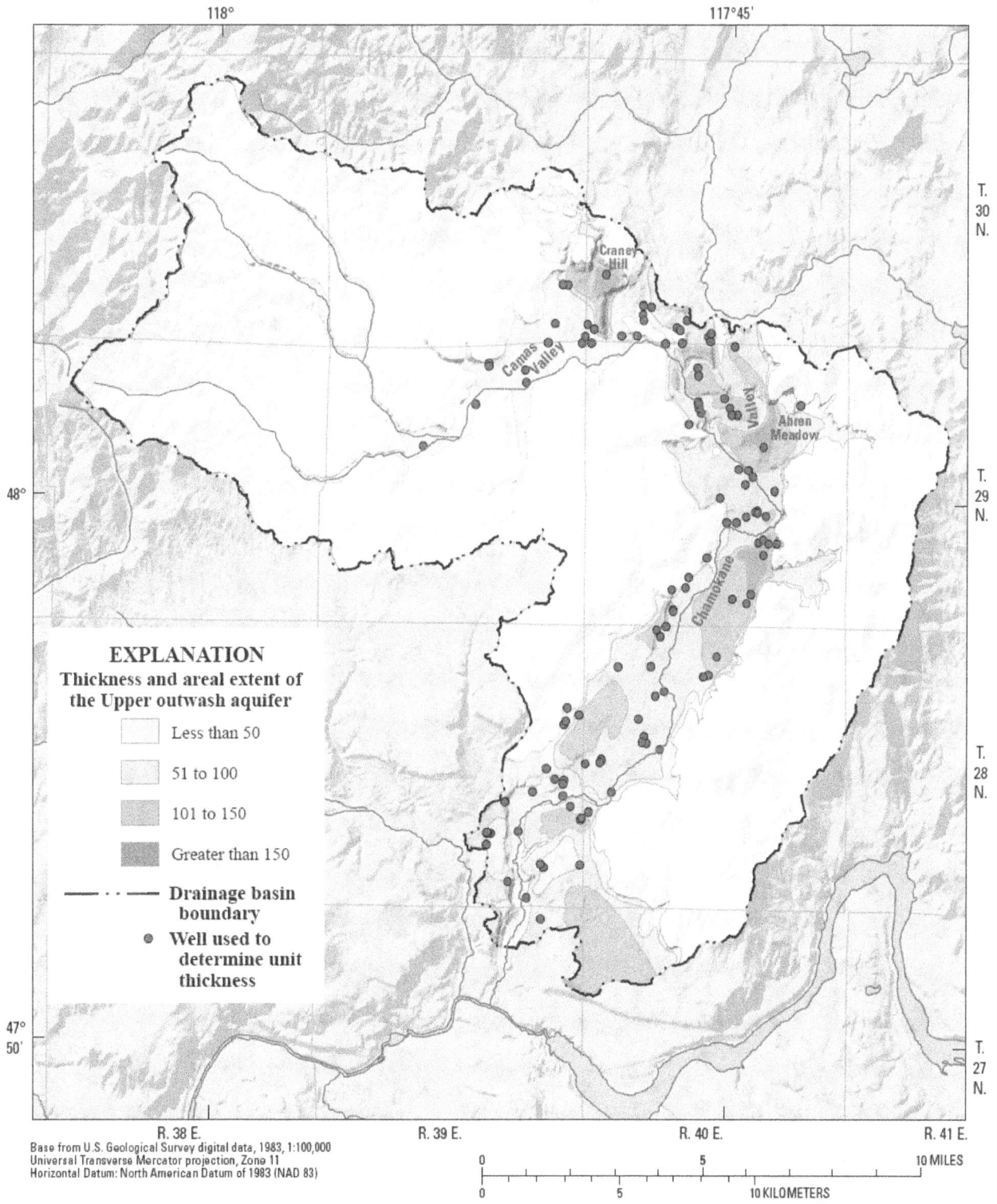

Figure 7. Thickness and areal extent of the Upper outwash aquifer in the Chamokane Creek basin, Stevens County, Washington.

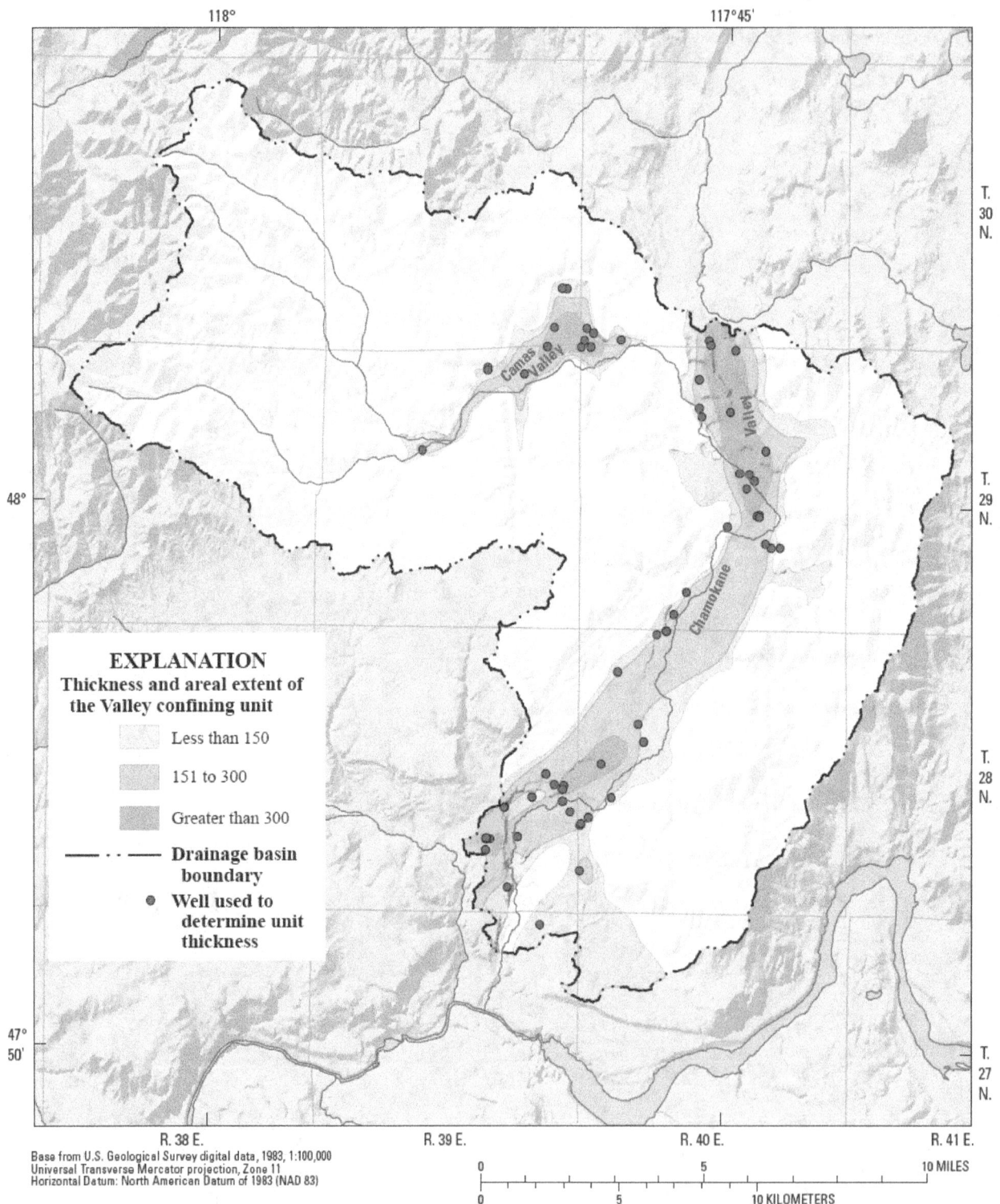

Figure 8.   Thickness and areal extent of the Valley confining unit in the Chamokane Creek basin, Stevens County, Washington.

Hydrogeologic Units

The Upper outwash aquifer (UA) of the Chamokane Creek basin is an unconfined aquifer consisting of sand, gravel, cobbles, and boulders, with minor silt and (or) clay interbeds. Previously described geologic units that comprise the bulk of this aquifer include glaciofluvial deposits (outwash), glacial outburst flood deposits, and alluvial deposits. Near Springdale, the aquifer includes till, a lower-permeability deposit comprised of compacted and poorly-sorted silt, sand, gravel, and cobbles with lenses of moderately sorted sand and gravel.

The Upper outwash aquifer occurs along the length of the Chamokane and Camas Valleys (fig. 6; pl. 1); 57 project wells are completed in this aquifer. Although the Upper outwash aquifer exists over much of the valley floors, some places within the aquifer are not sufficiently saturated to yield sustainable quantities of water to wells. Wells are drilled into deeper units in these areas. For example, most wells south of Ford are drilled into the Lower aquifer because the Upper aquifer in those areas yields insufficient quantities of water.

Thickness of the aquifer ranges from less than 50 ft along the margins of the unit to more than 150 ft where glacial terraces comprise the unit including the south side of Craney Hill and at the mouth of Ahren Meadow (fig. 7; pl. 2, sections B–B' and C–C'). From the Swamp Creek area southward through Walkers Prairie to near the mouth of the basin, the unit is extremely coarse-grained in most of the upper 20–30 ft where cobbles, boulders, and gravel are common. The lower part of the aquifer generally is composed of gravel and sand with few cobbles or boulders.

In the Camas Valley, where the Upper outwash aquifer is composed mostly of recent alluvial deposits along stream courses, it contains more sand and clay, and is therefore less productive than along Walkers Prairie. As illustrated on section A–A' (pl. 2), the aquifer is about 15–30 ft thick over much of the Camas Valley, but thickens to about 80 ft near the outlet of the valley near well 30N/40E-32P01. Although thick coarse-grained outwash deposits occur on the northern slopes of Camas Valley (fig. 7), they are not fully saturated; therefore, unreliable amounts of water generally are produced. For example, drillers noted nearly 300 ft of dry gravel and sand in well 30N/40E-30K01D1 before drilling into deeper more saturated material (pl. 2, section B–B').

The Landslide unit (LU) is composed of poorly sorted deposits of broken basalt and sedimentary interbeds of the Columbia River Basalt Group, covered in places by glacial deposits. Locally, the Landslide unit is an aquifer with variable yields and supplies water to nine of the project wells. The unit occurs along the eastern slopes of the basalt mesa on the eastern uplands of the Spokane Indian Reservation and on the western flanks of Happy Hill near Ford. The extent of this hydrogeologic unit at land surface corresponds to the geologic unit Qmw shown on plate 2. The approximate extent of this unit below land surface is shown on hydrogeologic sections D–D' through I–I' (pl. 2). As illustrated on the sections, the Landslide unit likely is in hydraulic connection with the Upper outwash aquifer along Walkers Prairie.

The Valley confining unit (VC) consists mostly of low-permeability glaciolacustrine silt and clay (Qla). The unit occurs at depth throughout the Camas and Chamokane Valleys and is continuous northward into the Colville Valley (fig. 8; pl. 2, section I–I'). Discontinuous lenses of sand or gravel within the unit contribute usable quantities of water to some wells; 16 of the project wells are completed in this unit (pl. 1; table 1). Coarse-grained lenses within the VC appear to be more common in the southern part of the basin where Missoula flood deposits following the Spokane River drainage are interbedded with the glaciolacustrine deposits (pl. 2, section G–G'). Thickness of the VC commonly is 150–300 ft along the Camas and Chamokane Valleys and exceeds 300 ft in the central Camas Valley, Swamp Creek area, and near Ford (fig. 8).

The Lower aquifer (LA) is a confined aquifer consisting of sand and some gravel that occurs at depth in the Camas and Chamokane Valleys below the Valley confining unit (pl. 2, sections A–A' through I–I'). Thirty of the project wells are completed in this unit (table 1, pl. 1). The Lower aquifer is continuous northward into the Colville Valley (pl. 2, section I–I'). The approximate southern extent of the Lower aquier is shown as being truncated near Chamokane Falls based on surficial outcrop of bedrock in that vicinity and well records that indicate the absence of a lower aquifer (pl. 2, southern end of I–I'; fig. 10). The Chamokane basin Lower aquifer does not appear to be connnected with similar deposits along the Spokane River. The thickness of LA is not well known. Only two project wells, 28N/39E-23P01 (pl. 2, section I–I') and 28N/40E-17C01 (pl. 2, sections F–F' and I–I'), fully penetrate the Lower aquifer and reach the underlying Bedrock unit. At these two wells, the thickness of the Lower aquifer was interpreted to be 125 ft and 138 ft, respectively.

The Basalt unit (BT) is composed of Columbia River Basalt, a dense, dark basalt with generally fine-grained interbeds. Locally, coarse-grained interbeds occur in the unit west of Springdale. Water from cracks and fractures in the basalt and from zones between lava flows supplied 18 of the project wells (table 1, pl. 1). The Basalt unit occurs at land surface in the eastern uplands of the Spokane Indian Reservation and on Lyons Hill and Craney Hill (pl. 2). This hydrogeologic unit includes Miocene basalt (Mb) overlain by thin and discontinuous Quaternary loess (Qlo) and glacial deposits (Qgu). The thickness of the unit in the Chamokane Creek basin is largely unknown. One project well, 28N/39E-36D01, penetrated 253 ft of basalt before reaching the underlying granite (pl. 2, section H–H').

The Bedrock unit (BR) includes argillite, conglomerate, dolomite, gneiss, schist, slate, quartzite, shale, limestone, and granite. The unit locally yields usable quantities of water where rocks are fractured. Nineteen project wells obtain their water from this unit. Yields generally are small and numerous abandoned wells are in the unit. The Bedrock hydrogeologic unit includes geologic unit Tybr and thin and discontinuous Qal, Qlo, and Qgf that overly the bedrock.

Horizontal Hydraulic Conductivity

Hydraulic conductivity is a measure of a material's ability to transmit water. In unconsolidated sediment, it is dependent on the size, shape, distribution, and packing of the particles. These characteristics vary within each hydrogeologic unit and hydraulic conductivity values vary correspondingly.

Horizontal hydraulic conductivity was estimated for the hydrogeologic units using the drawdown/discharge relation reported on drillers' logs that reported pump testing wells for 1–6.5 hours. Only data from those wells with a driller's log containing discharge rate, duration of pumping, drawdown, static water level, well-construction data, and lithologic log were used.

Two methods were used to estimate hydraulic conductivity, depending on well construction. For data from wells with a screened or perforated interval, the modified Theis equation (Ferris and others, 1962) was first used to estimate transmissivity of the pumped interval. Transmissivity is the product of horizontal hydraulic conductivity and thickness of the hydrogeologic unit supplying water to the well.

The modified equation is

$$s = \frac{Q}{4\pi T} \ln \frac{2.25Tt}{r^2 S} \tag{1}$$

where
    s = drawdown in the well, in feet;
    Q = discharge, or pumping rate, of the well, in cubic feet per day;
    T = transmissivity of the hydrogeologic unit, in square feet per day;
    t = length of time the well was pumped, in days;
    r = radius of the well, in feet; and
    S = storage coefficient, a dimensionless number, assumed to be 0.0001 for confined units and 0.1 for unconfined units.

Assumptions for using equation 1 are that aquifers are homogeneous, isotropic, and infinite in extent; wells are fully penetrating; flow to the well is horizontal; and water is released from storage instantaneously. Additionally, for unconfined aquifers, drawdown is assumed to be small in relation to the saturated thickness of the aquifer. Although many of the assumptions are not precisely met, the field conditions in the study area approximate most of the assumptions.

A computer program was used to solve equation 1 for transmissivity (T) using Newton's iterative method (Carnahan and others, 1969). The calculated transmissivity values were not sensitive to assumed storage coefficient values; the difference in computed transmissivity between using 0.1 and 0.0001 for the storage coefficent is a factor of only about 2. The following equation was used to calculate horizontal hydraulic conductivity from the calculated transmissivity:

$$K_h = \frac{T}{b} \tag{2}$$

where
    K_h = horizontal hydraulic conductivity of the geologic material near the well opening, in feet per day; and
    b = thickness, in feet, approximated using the length of the open interval as reported in the driller's report.

The use of the length of a well's open interval for b overestimates values of K_h because the equations assume that all the water flows horizontally within a layer of this thickness. Although some of the flow will be outside this interval, the amount may be relatively small because in most sedimentary deposits, vertical flow is inhibited by layering.

For data from wells having only an open ended casing (no perforations), a second equation was used to estimate hydraulic conductivities. Bear (1979) provides an equation for hemispherical flow to an open-ended well just penetrating a hydrogeologic unit. When modified for spherical flow to an open-ended well within a unit, the equation becomes

$$K_h = \frac{Q}{4\pi s r} \tag{3}$$

Equation 3 is based on the assumption that horizontal and vertical hydraulic conductivities are equal, which is not likely for the deposits in the study area. The result of violating this assumption is underestimating K_h by an unknown amount.

Hydraulic conductivity data are summarized by hydrogeologic unit in the following table. Data were unavailable for the Landslide and Bedrock units. The median values of estimated hydraulic conductivities for the aquifers are similar in magnitude to values reported by Freeze and Cherry (1979) for similar materials: Upper outwash aquifer, 540 ft/d and Lower aquifer, 19 ft/d. The medians of estimated hydraulic conductivities for the Valley confining unit (10 ft/d), and the Basalt unit (3.7 ft/d) are higher than is typical for most of the material in these units because the data for confining units usually are from zones where lenses of coarse material exist and, in the case of the Basalt unit, where fractures or sedimentary interbeds exist. As a result, the data are biased toward the more productive zones in these units and are not representative of the entire unit. The minimum hydraulic conductivities for the hydrogeologic units illustrate that there are zones of low hydraulic conductivity in most units. Additionally, the range of hydraulic conductivities is at least three orders of magnitude for most units, indicating substantial heterogeneity and inherent uncertainty in estimating hydraulic conductivity.

Hydrogeologic unit	Estimated hydraulic conductivity (feet per day)			
	Minimum	Median	Maximum	Number of values
Upper outwash aquifer	15	540	7,900	10
Valley confining unit	2	10	860	4
Lower aquifer	4	19	3,000	8
Basalt unit	.93	3.7	6.5	2

Estimates of horizontal hydraulic conductivity reported in several other investigations provide useful comparisons to the values estimated during this investigation. Buchanan and others (1988) reported an average horizontal hydraulic conductivity of 2,664 ft/d for the Upper outwash aquifer of Walkers Prairie based on a long-term pump test with multiple observation wells. On the Dawn millsite south of Ford, the horizontal hydraulic conductivity of the Upper outwash aquifer was estimated to be 14–140 ft/d based on pump test data (Washington Department of Health, 1991). Golder Associates, Inc. (2008) reported an average horizontal hydraulic conductivity of 331 ft/d for the Lower aquifer near the southern end of Chamokane Creek basin based on specific capacity data. Horizontal hydraulic conductivity of the Lower aquifer near Galbraith Springs is approximately 1,300 ft/day, based on a pump test conducted by Rittenhouse-Zeman and Associates, Inc. (1989). Whiteman and others (1994) estimated the median hydraulic conductivity of the Grande Ronde Basalt over the Columbia Plateau as 4.9ft/d based on specific capacity data.

Although many uncertainties are in the estimated values of hydraulic conductivity, these estimates provide an initial assessment of the relative differences in hydraulic conductivity between the different hydrogeologic units. These relative differences provide the basis for an initial conceptual model of hydraulic conductivity values to be used in the GSFLOW model; these values will be refined during model calibration.

Yield and Specific Capacity

A summary of well yields, as reported on drillers' logs used during this investigation, is shown in table 3 by hydrogeologic unit. Well-yield testing is done to determine if an adequate and sustainable yield is available from a well. Driller-reported well yields are not only dependent on the productivity of the unit to which the well is open, but also is a function of the design and purpose of the well. During well-yield testing, a well intended for municipal purposes likely would be pumped at a higher rate and have a larger diameter casing and a longer open interval than one intended for single-family use, thereby having an apparent higher yield than that for the single-family well. Despite the fact that yields often are estimates, they are useful in comparing the general productivity of hydrogeologic units; they also illustrate the variability within a single unit. Based on the data set used for this study, the median yields for the Upper outwash aquifer, the Landslide unit, the Valley confining unit, the Lower aquifer, the Basalt unit, and the Bedrock unit are 25, 45, 10, 55, 11, and 3 gal/min, respectively.

A summary of specific capacity information, derived from driller-reported yield divided by the drawdown measured in the well during pumping, is shown in the table below, by hydrogeologic unit. Specific capacity often is used to describe the productivity of a hydrogeologic unit. Based on the data set used for this study, the median specific capacity for the Upper outwash aquifer, the Valley confining unit, the Lower aquifer, and the Basalt unit are 7.6, 1.7, 0.62, and 0.18 (gal/min)/ft, respectively. Specific capacity is expected to be smaller for confined aquifers than unconfined aquifers (Freeze and Cherry, 1979).

Table 3. Summary of yield and specific capacity for hydrogeologic units in the Chamokane Creek basin, Stevens County, Washington.

[0 indicates dry well. **Abbreviations:** gal/min, gallon per minute; (gal/min)/ft, gallon per minute per foot; –, no data]

Hydrogeologic unit	Yield (gal/min)				Specific capacity ([gal/min]/ft)			
	Minimum	Median	Maximum	Number of values	Minimum	Median	Maximum	Number of values
Upper outwash aquifer	0	25	2,000	49	0.7	7.6	190	8
Landslide unit	15	45	100	9	–	–	–	–
Valley confining unit	0	10	38	14	.07	1.7	15	4
Lower aquifer	2	55	400	32	.12	.62	4.1	7
Basalt unit	2	11	40	16	.15	.18	.21	2
Bedrock unit	.25	3	20	18	–	–	–	–

Occurrence and Movement of Groundwater

Recharge

Direct precipitation recharges the Upper outwash aquifer over its extent and streamflow recharges the aquifer where losing stream reaches directly overlie the aquifer. Significant mountain-front recharge also may occur along the perimeter of the aquifer where it is in contact with Landslide unit deposits or productive zones within the Basalt or Bedrock hydrogeologic units. Recharge to the Upper outwash aquifer from streams is discussed in detail later in this report. Recharge from precipitation and other sources will be estimated in Phase 2 of this investigation.

Recharge to the Lower aquifer likely occurs in several areas. Water-level data indicate that recharge occurs from near Springdale through the Swamp Creek area where vertical head gradients between the Upper and Lower aquifers generally are downward. Localized recharge also occurs along the walls of the Camas Valley and Walkers Prairie where coarse talus slopes and landslide deposits along basalt bluffs or glacial outwash fans overlie and interfinger with the otherwise continuous Valley confining unit.

Groundwater Flow Directions

To estimate directions of horizontal groundwater flow, water-level maps were drawn for the Upper outwash aquifer and the Lower aquifer. Contours of equal water-level altitudes were manually drawn at convenient intervals, using approximate linear interpretation between point measurements, topographic map contours, and stream-surface altitudes where appropriate. The directions of flow were inferred to be from higher to lower water levels and perpendicular to water-level contours where data were sufficient to draw contours. Groundwater levels measured during the well inventory (autumn 2007) were used to construct the water-level maps.

Horizontal groundwater flow in the Upper outwash aquifer generally mimics the surface-water drainage pattern of the basin. Groundwater flow moves from the topographically high tributary-basin areas toward the topographically lower valley floors (fig. 9). Over the entire basin, water-level altitudes in the Upper outwash aquifer range from 2,150 ft in the Camas Valley to 1,760 ft near Ford. The general distribution of horizontal gradients was about 13–50 ft/mi in the Camas Valley, about 80 ft/mi where Chamokane Creek exits Icebox Canyon to near its confluence with Swamp Creek, 20–30 ft/mi from south of Springdale through the Swamp

Creek area, and 12–16 ft/mi along Walkers Prairie. The smallest gradient in the Upper outwash aquifer, about 12 ft/mi, was measured along Walkers Prairie.

Horizontal groundwater flow in the Lower aquifer is south to southwest from near Springdale to south of Ford (fig. 10). Along the Chamokane Valley floor, water-level altitudes within the Lower aquifer range from 1,885 ft near Swamp Creek to 1,600 ft near the lower end of the basin. Horizontal gradients are about 20 ft/mi along Walkers Prairie but increase to between 80 and 200 ft/mi from near Ford to the southern extent of the Lower aquifer where the unit thins or pinches out (fig. 10). In the Camas Valley, horizontal groundwater flow is to the east and water-level altitudes range from about 2,150 to less than 2,050 ft with a horizontal gradient of about 100 ft/mi.

The location of the groundwater divide for the Lower aquifer is near the surface-water divide for the basin, near Springdale, Wash. (fig. 10). Its location was determined by measuring water levels in Lower aquifer wells north and south of the surface-water divide in the Colville River and Chamokane Creek basins, respectively. The groundwater divide is approximately mid-way between two 1,885 ft waterlevel altitude contours, one in the Colville River basin and one in the Chamokane Creek basin (fig. 10).

Directions of vertical flow were inferred from water-level altitudes in the Upper outwash aquifer and the Lower aquifer where the units overlie one another. Water-level altitudes in closely spaced wells also were reviewed to assess if vertical gradients could be determined. In wells 29N/40E-09G03 and 09G02 downstream of Icebox Canyon and upstream of Swamp Creek (pl. 1), the difference in water levels was almost 60 ft, with a downward gradient from the Upper outwash aquifer to the underlying Lower aquifer. Conversely, in wells 29N/40E-15R02 and 15Q02 about 2 m farther downgradient, the difference in water levels was about 20 ft, with an upward gradient from the Lower aquifer to the overlying Upper outwash aquifer. In wells 28N/40E-05A01 and 05A02 (pl. 1), the difference in water levels was about 4 ft, again with an upward gradient from the Lower aquifer to the overlying Upper outwash aquifer. Based on available water-level data, vertical flow in the basin generally is downward in the high-altitude areas of the side basins and near Swamp Creek. Vertical flow along Walkers Prairie generally is upward. In the Camas Valley, an upward vertical head gradient exists at flowing well 29N/39E-02J01, but at wells 30N/40E-31N01 and 29N/40E-06D01, the difference in water levels was about 90 ft, with a downward gradient from the Valley confining unit to the Lower aquifer. Flowing well 28N/39E-24K01, near the mouth of the Chamokane Creek basin, indicates upward flow from the Valley confining unit to the overlying Upper outwash aquifer.

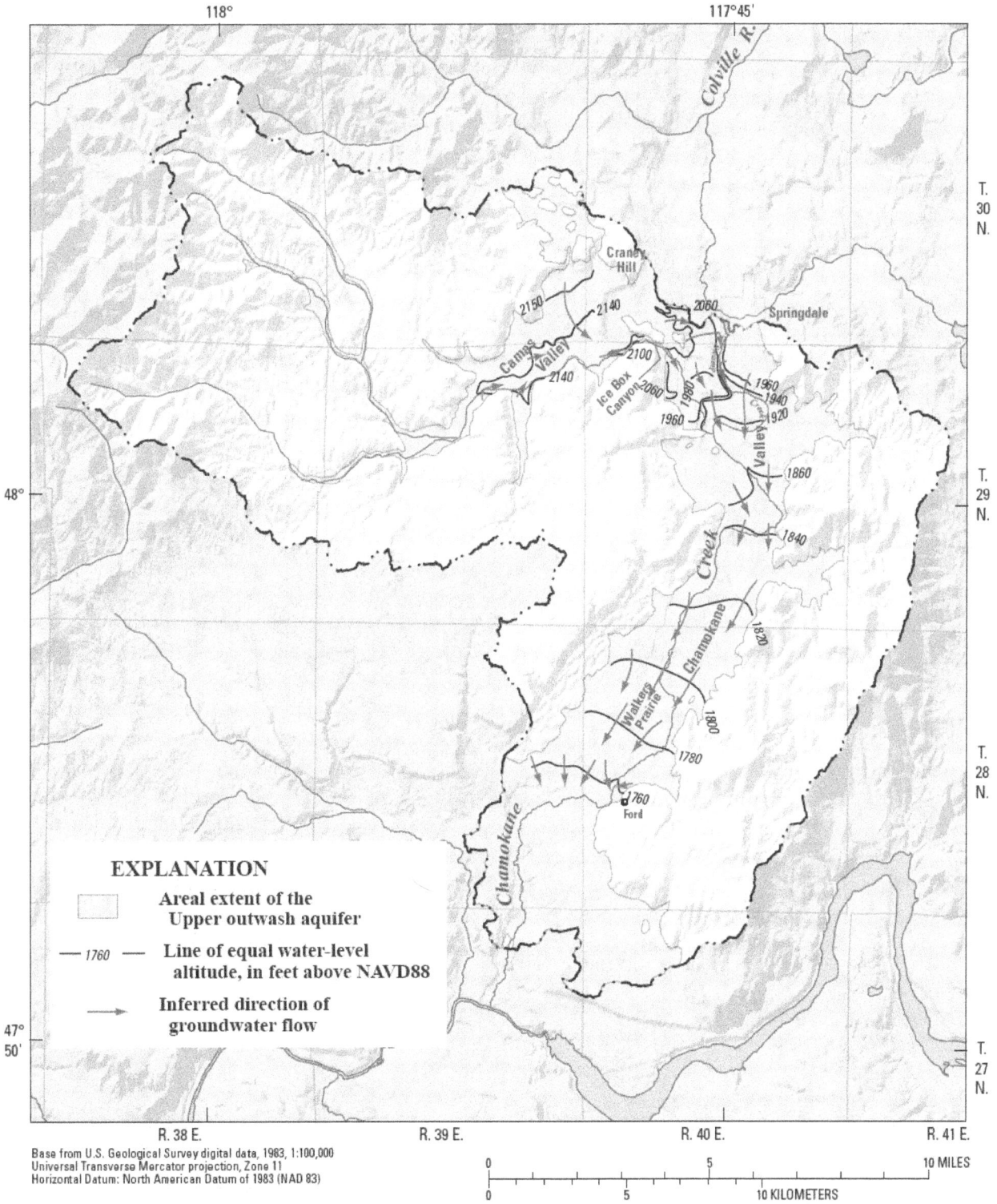

Figure 9.   Areal extent, water-level altitudes, and inferred directions of groundwater flow in the Upper outwash aquifer in the Chamokane Creek basin, Stevens County, Washington.

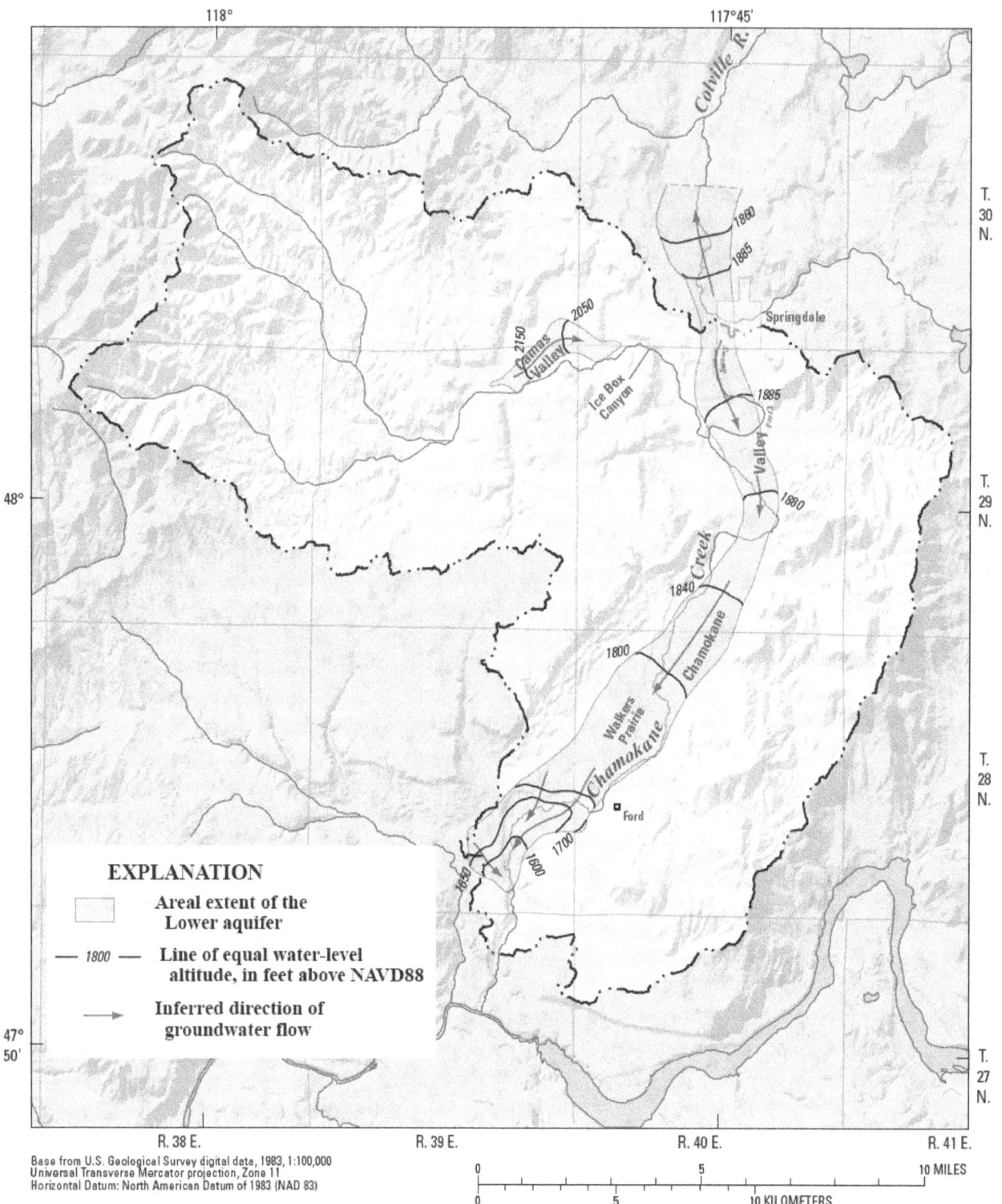

Figure 10.   Areal extent, water-level altitudes, and inferred directions of groundwater flow in the Lower aquifer in the Chamokane Creek basin, Stevens County, Washington.

Groundwater Discharge

Discharge from the Upper outwash aquifer occurs mostly as pumping from wells and at springs and seeps. A line of springs and seeps along an arcuate bluff west of Ford represents the major discharge zone of the Upper outwash aquifer (pl. 1). Outflow from this region supports year-round flow in Chamokane Creek downstream of Ford. Springs discharging from the Upper outwash aquifer along Swamp Creek and between Icebox Canyon and the confluence of Chamokane and Swamp Creeks (pl. 1) support streamflow in those stream reaches. Just downstream, however, surface-flow in the stream disappears during much of the year near the northeast corner of the Spokane Indian Reservation. Discharge from the Lower aquifer occurs as pumping from wells and, in areas of upward flow gradients, as discharge to overlying hydrogeologic units. In Camas Valley, one flowing well, 29N/39E-02J01, discharges at land surface. At the east end of Camas Valley, groundwater flow likely discharges into overlying sediments and Chamokane Creek near the head of Icebox Canyon. Similarly, discharge at the lower end of the basin, south of Ford, may be upward through overlying units and ultimately into Chamokane Creek.

Seasonal Variations in Groundwater Levels

Median water-level altitudes measured during the synoptic measurements in spring 2008 (March 24–April 1, 2008) generally were slightly higher than those measured during the synoptic measurements in autumn 2007. The following table summarizes the differences in water levels between autumn 2007 and spring 2008 by hydrogeologic unit.

Hydrogeologic unit	Difference in water level altitude (feet)			
	Minimum	Median	Maximum	Number of values
Upper outwash aquifer	-1.5	0.15	7.57	29
Landslide unit	-2.58	.20	15.05	6
Valley confining unit	-.79	.90	3.24	4
Lower aquifer	-1.94	.04	5.94	15
Basalt unit	-.3	2.37	5.28	6
Bedrock unit	-1.83	-.61	2.85	5

Due to higher than usual snow fall and continued freezing temperatures in early 2008, however, the spring 2008 synoptic measurements were made before water-level altitudes reached their spring maximums based on subsequent monthly measurements. Therefore, the maximum seasonal variation in water-level altitudes was better documented by the monitoring-well network where monthly depth-to-water measurements were made from March 2008 to December 2009.

The first rise on the hydrographs (generally from autumn 2007 or winter 2008 through June 2008) shows that in the Upper outwash aquifer, water level altitudes commonly rose from about 2 to nearly 10 ft (see hydrographs for wells 28N/40E-17J01, 28N/40E-05A01, 29N/40E-15R02, and 29N/40E-23M06; pl. 1). The highest water-level altitudes in the Upper outwash aquifer occurred about 5–6 months after peak winter precipitation (snowfall reported as water equivalent) was measured at the AgriMet station in December 2007, and 1–3 months after peak discharge was recorded downstream of Chamokane Falls (pl. 1). The second rise on the hydrographs generally was several feet less than the first, corresponding to less precipitation in December 2008 through January 2009 compared to the previous year (pl. 1). The combined data set for this study indicate that peak snowfall occurred in December; snowmelt and, therefore, stream discharge peaked in April and groundwater levels in the Upper outwash aquifer then peaked about 1–3 months later after streamflow infiltration passed through the unsaturated zone and recharged the shallow aquifer.

Water-level altitudes in the Lower aquifer rose about 3–4 ft in the first season (see hydrographs for wells 28N/39E-26E01, 28N/40E-17C01, and 28N/40E-05A02; pl. 1) and slightly less the second season. Similar to water levels in the Upper outwash aquifer, the highest water-level altitudes in the Lower aquifer occurred about 5–6 months after the highest precipitation.

The paired hydrographs for closely spaced wells, one completed in the Upper outwash aquifer and one completed in the Lower aquifer, indicate nearly identical timing of the seasonal rise and falls in water levels (wells 28N/40E-05A01 and 05A02, 28N/40E-17J01 and 17C01, and 29N/40E-15R02 and 15Q02; pl. 1). The Upper aquifer water levels exhibited a slightly greater seasonal fluctuation, particularly in well 28N/40E-17J01, than the Lower aquifer water levels. This was expected given the unconfined nature of the Upper aquifer and its close proximity to recharge from losing stream reaches and from precipitation. The overall similarity of fluctuations in water levels in the Upper outwash aquifer and the Lower aquifer indicates that these aquifers may be well connected despite the apparently continuous Valley confining unit that separates them.

Long term (1959–2007) water-level and precipitation records indicate similar relations between groundwater levels and precipitation as those measured during this study (2007–09). Figure 11 shows long term water-level elevations for three wells (28N/40E-17J01, 28N/40E-08H02, and 28N/40E-28P01) and long term precipitation for the Wellpinit, Washington station, the closest long term weather station to the basin. Water levels have been measured in six wells, including the three listed above, by Chamokane Water Masters from 1971 to present (2010) (James Lyerla, Chamokane Water Master, written commun., 2007). Additionally, water levels were measured in well 28N/40E-17J01 bimonthly from 1957 to1980 by the U.S. Geological Survey. Precipitation has been measured at the Wellpinit station from1923 to present (2010) and monthly totals for 1923–2007 are available through the Western Regional Climate Center (2010). The long-term trends of water-level altitudes follow climatic variability well without apparent long-term changes in water-levels (fig. 11).

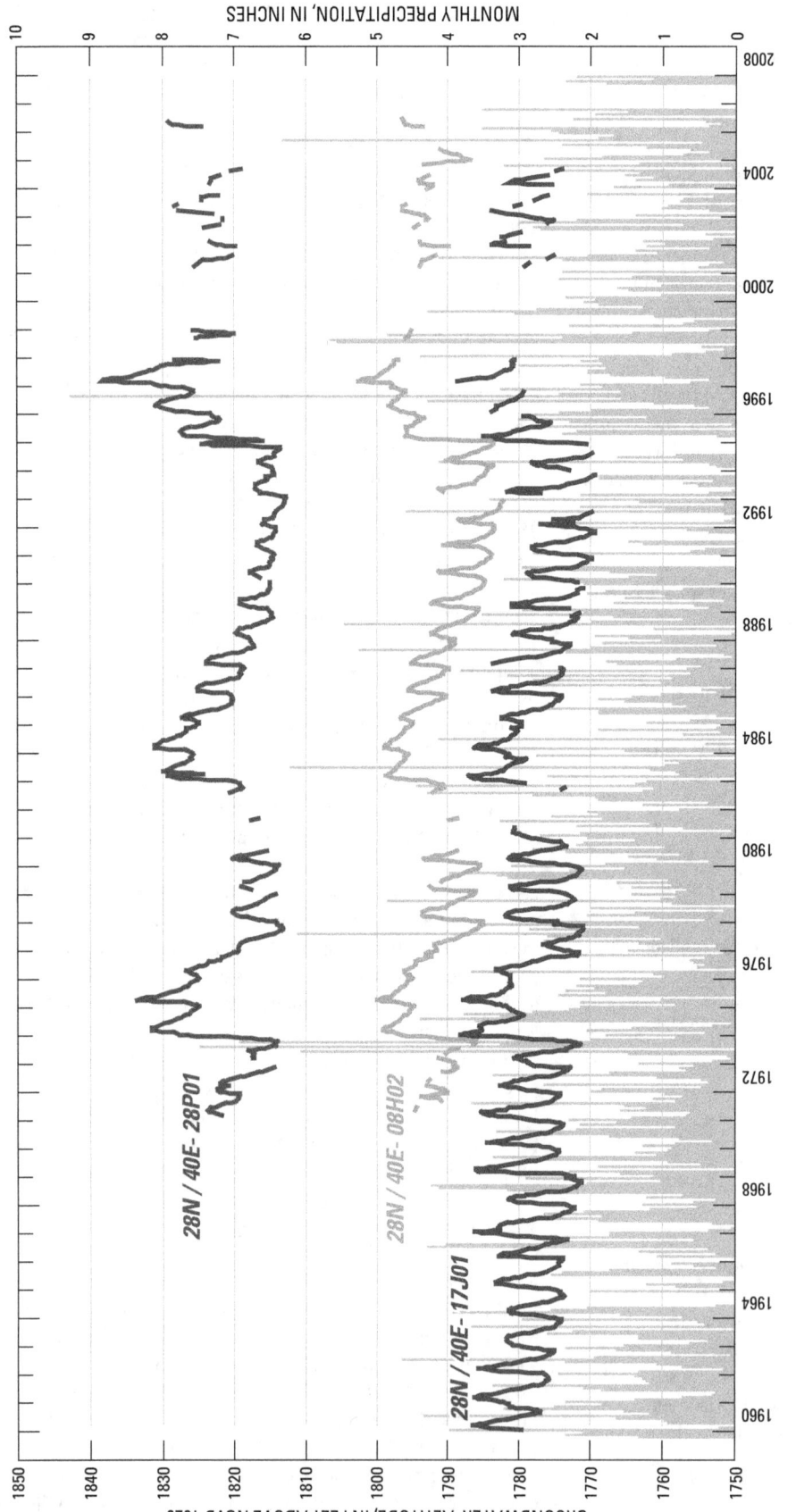

Figure 11.   Long-term groundwater-level altitudes in Chamokane Creek basin and precipitation for Wellpinit, Washington station.

Surface-Water System

Historical Streamflow

Historical streamflow records are available for one active USGS gaging station, Chamokane Creek below Falls near Long Lake (12433200) and one discontinued gaging station Chamokane Creek near Springdale(12433100). Mean annual discharge near the mouth of the basin at Chamokane Creek below Falls near Long Lake was 62.5 ft³/s for the 28 years when a complete record was available (1972–1978 and 1988–2008).

Snowmelt is the primary source of runoff in the watershed; rainfall is the secondary source of runoff and occasionally contributes to peak flows as rain-on-snow events. Mountain altitudes, even in the Huckleberry Mountains where the Chamokane Creek headwaters originate, are less than 5,000 ft and the annual snowpack normally is entirely melted by mid-June. Peak flows from snowmelt commonly occur from March to mid-April; 20 of 28 recorded annual peak flows at Chamokane Creek below Falls near Long Lake occurred in March or April (table 4). The mean daily discharge at the gaging station typically reaches its low point by late July and remains low into October (fig. 12). Flows increase only slightly in October and early November due to autumn rains, but can increase significantly in December with the arrival of winter storms and greater precipitation.

The three headwater branches, the North Fork Chamokane Creek, the Middle Fork Chamokane Creek, and the South Fork Chamokane Creek, which form the main stem of Chamokane Creek are all intermittent in their upper reaches. Chamokane Creek becomes perennial most years in Camas Valley and remains so until it reaches the Walkers Prairie area where it again becomes intermittent due to seasonal infiltration losses through the channel bed.

Springs

Springs are an important component of the Chamokane surface-water system and sustain much of the flow during the usually dry months of July to November. Groundwater discharges at a series of large springs at the southern end of Walkers Prairie along an east–west oriented bluff beginning just west of the town of Ford. Much of this hillside seeps water in places causing the stream channel to have swampy reaches. Larger outflows occur at the Dawn Mining Company spring, the Washington Department of Fish and Wildlife spring, the

Table 4. Annual peak discharge for U.S. Geological Survey streamflow-gaging station 12433200, Chamokane Creek below Falls near Long Lake, Stevens County, Washington.

[**Abbreviation:** ft³/s, cubic feet per second]

Water year	Peak discharge (ft³/s)	Date
1972	332	02-29-72
1973	353	03-02-73
1974	1,430	01-16-74
1975	2,200	04-25-75
1976	316	04-09-76
1977	44	11-21-76
1978	326	03-24-78
1988	165	04-03-88
1989	435	03-14-89
1990	210	06-02-90
1991	250	04-06-91
1992	164	01-29-92
1993	661	03-24-93
1994	133	03-19-94
1995	1,140	03-12-95
1996	873	04-24-96
1997	1,810	03-20-97
1998	555	03-24-98
1999	1,110	02-26-99
2000	753	03-05-00
2001	90	03-20-01
2002	743	01-09-02
2003	992	03-16-03
2004	115	03-19-04
2005	401	03-28-05
2006	1,240	01-11-06
2007	712	03-13-07
2008	625	04-15-08

Spokane Tribal Woodworks site, and the Galbraith Springs by the Spokane Tribal Fish Hatchery (pl. 1). Chamokane Creek is perennial downstream of these spring discharges and remains so, gaining water from the aquifer, for the rest of its course until its confluence with the Spokane River.

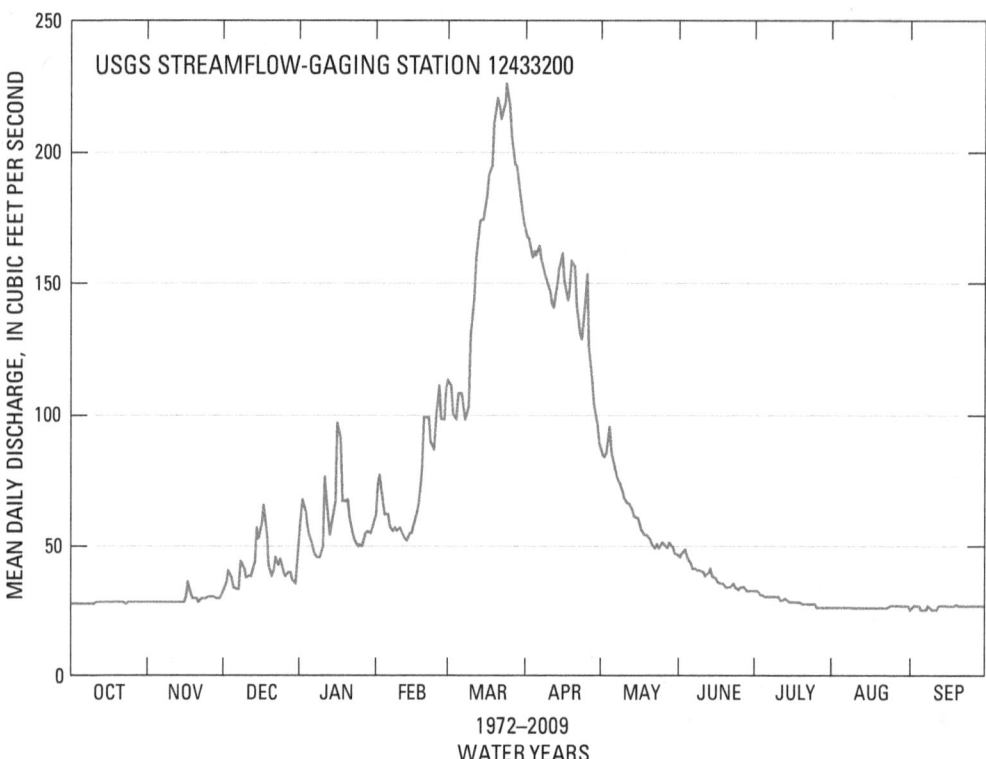

Figure 12.   Mean daily discharge for the period of record (1972–2009) for U.S. Geological Survey streamflow-gaging station 12433200, Chamokane Creek below Falls near Long Lake, Stevens County, Washington.

Measuring the discharge of these springs is difficult because they are mostly in an area with widespread seepage and lack distinct boundaries. Total outflows from the Washington Department of Fish and Wildlife (WDFW) and the Tribal Fish Hatchery include some groundwater pumped from wells to supplement natural spring water used at these sites, which then becomes return water. Outflow at Galbraith Springs (12433187) and the outflow downstream of the Tribal Fish Hatchery (12433190), which includes Galbraith Springs and all return flow from the hatchery, were measured concurrently during three synoptic measurement sets as part of this study (tables 5–7). Measured discharge from the Tribal Fish Hatchery was 7.76 ft³/s on October 11, 2007, and 9.87 ft³/s on April 17, 2008. The Stevens County Conservation District measured total outflow at the WDFW and the Spokane Fish Hatchery 27 times between November 1997 and March 1999. At the State hatchery, measurements ranged from a low of 6.1 ft³/s on January 5, 1998, to a high of 16.3 ft³/s on March 16, 1998. Measurements at the tribal hatchery

ranged from a low of 3.0 ft³/s on January 5, 1998, to a high of 15.3 ft³/s on March 29, 1999 (C. Kessler, Stevens County Conservation District, written commun., 2009).

The most complete attempt to measure the springs discharge was in 1987 (Wozniewicz, 1989). Measuring stations were established at the north (upgradient) end of the springs region downstream of the Ford bridge (near station 24; pl. 1), and at the south (downgradient) end just downstream of the confluence between Galbraith Springs and Chamokane Creek. Measurements were made at these stations and at all the major springs between stations during the low flow period from late July 1987 to late October 1987. The average total discharge of springs and seeps between the north and south measuring stations was 20.9 ft³/s and an additional average discharge of 2.0 ft³/s was calculated for springs and seeps between the south station and the USGS gaging station at Chamokane Creek below Falls near Long Lake (Wozniewicz, 1989).

Swamp Creek is the only tributary to Chamokane Creek that is perennial; all other tributaries are intermittent. Swamp Creek differs from the other tributaries in that it does not originate in the highlands. Swamp Creek is spring fed and begins in a swampy area just west of the town of Springdale. Thomas Creek also is spring fed and flows southeast out of the hills at the western edge of Walkers Prairie (pl. 1), but terminates in a pond on the floodplain that appears to have no surface-water outlet. Tributaries other than Swamp Creek reach Chamokane Creek as surface flow only during the spring snowmelt season and for short periods after significant rainfall events.

Streamflow Gains and Losses

Three sets of synoptic discharge measurements were made at 28 sites along Chamokane Creek and its tributaries during this study (pl. 1) to identify gaining and losing reaches and to describe how surface water moves through the basin during high- and low-flow conditions. A gaining reach is where streamflow increases due to inflow of groundwater. A losing reach is where streamflow decreases due to outflow of water through the streambed into the ground. Two low-flow measurements were made during late summer or early autumn of 2007 and 2008, and are referred to as seepage runs that represent approximately steady-flow conditions. One set of high-flow synoptic discharge measurements was made in April 2008. For simplicity, the surface-water measuring sites are referred to by sequential map numbers (1–28) in the following text and on pl. 1 (tables 5–7 list full station names and eight-digit USGS gaging station numbers).

Tributaries in the Chamokane Creek basin are known to be intermittent with little if any surface flow reaching Chamokane Creek during the summer and autumn low-flow period. Therefore, tributary measuring sites were selected closer to their headwaters than the confluence with Chamokane Creek to minimize the number of dry channel locations. Because of their upstream locations, streamflow gain and loss data from many tributary measuring sites may not be representative of gains or losses along the main stem of Chamokane Creek. Additionally, although none were reported or observed, atypical activities occurring during a measurement, such as exceptionally high, short-term pumping from a near-stream well could affect the measurements.

Furthermore, gains or losses of streamflow, as described in this report, refer to the cumulative or net gain or loss in streamflow between two measurement sites. It was beyond the scope of this study to locate and measure every tributary and surface-water diversion and return, so the reported losses and gains in streamflow may be due to processes other than groundwater/surface-water interactions.

The first seepage run was completed in late September and early October 2007 to characterize low-flow streamflow conditions (table 5). Discharge was measured at most of the same sites during subsequent measurements made in 2008. Selected sites were not revisited. Site 12433060 (Unnamed Tributary Site 1 off Mickelson Road near Springdale) had no flow when visited on October 5, 2007, and was discontinued after better measuring conditions were determined at nearby site 12433062 (Unnamed Tributary Site 2 off Mickelson Road) on the same day. Site 12433048 (Unnamed Tributary at Bowler Road near Springdale) had no flow during the 2007 and 2008 seepage runs and was not included in the April 2008 high-flow measurement set.

A review of long-term data for the Chamokane Creek below Falls gaging station indicates that the long term (1970–2008) daily mean flows are 27 and 29 ft^3/s for September and October, respectively. This is nearly identical to the daily mean values of 27 and 28 ft^3/s for September and October 2007. The similarity of long term mean flow and flow during the synoptic low-flow period implies that conditions at the time of the measurements were representative of typical conditions.

Results of the 2007 seepage run indicate that no flow (or little flow) was observed throughout the upper reaches of Chamokane Creek, including the headwaters and Camas Valley sections. The only tributary in this section where any significant flow was measured was at site 12433067 (Unnamed Tributary above Drum Road near Springdale) where flow was 0.18 ft^3/s. Flow measured at site 12433075 (Chamokane Creek above Swamp Creek near Springdale) was 1.02 ft^3/s. No flow or minimal flow was measured in the Walkers Prairie area with no flow observed at site 12433100 (Chamokane Creek near Springdale). Measured discharge at Chamokane Creek at Ford-Wellpinit Road (site 12433175) was 1.26 ft^3/s on September 20, 2007. On the same date, discharge at Chamokane Creek below Falls near Long Lake (site 12433200) was 28 ft^3/s (table 5).

Table 5.   Seepage investigation, Chamokane Creek, Spokane River basin, Stevens County, Washington, September 18–October 11, 2007.

[**Map No**. shown on plate 1. A series of discharge measurements were made September 18–October 11, 2007, on Chamokane Creek and some of its tributaries to study gains and losses (modified from U.S. Geological Survey, 2007). The reach covered 30.7 miles. River mile 31.8 is the confluence of Little Chamokane Creek and Spokane River; river mile 32.5 is the confluence of Chamokane Creek and Spokane River. **Site name and location:** Site names in **bold** are on the main stem of Chamokane Creek. Indented sites are tributary to the next listed site. **Abbreviations**: ft³/s, cubic foot per second; C, degrees Celsius; –, no data]

Map No.	Site name and location	Measured discharge (ft³/s)	Date	Net gain or loss (ft³/s)	Water temperature (°C)
1	Middle Fork Chamokane Creek near Springdale (12433020)	0	09-18-07	–	–
2	South Fork Chamokane Creek near Springdale (12433030)	0	09-18-07	–	–
3	**Chamokane Creek below Forks, near Springdale (12433035)**	0	09-18-07	–	–
4	Unnamed Tributary at Rose Hill Road, near Springdale (12433040)	0	09-18-07	–	–
5	Unnamed Tributary at Springdale-Hunters Highway, near Springdale (12433043)	0	09-18-07	–	–
6	Unnamed Tributary at Bowler Road, near Springdale (12433048)	0	09-20-07	–	–
7	**Chamokane Creek at West Lyons Hill Road, near Springdale (12433055)**	0	09-20-07	–	–
8	Unnamed Tributary Site 1 off Mickelson Road, near Springdale (12433060)	0	10-05-07	–	–
9	Unnamed Tributary Site 2 off Mickelson Road, near Springdale (12433062)	.02	10-05-07	–	7.7
10	Unnamed Tributary above Drum Road, near Springdale (12433067)	.18	10-11-07	–	7.5
11	**Chamokane Creek at East Lyons Hill Road, near Springdale (12433070)**	.01	09-19-07	[1]-0.19	7.6
12	**Chamokane Creek above Swamp Creek, near Springdale (12433075)**	1.02	09-19-07	+1.01	11.5
13	Swamp Creek at Cemetery Road, near Springdale (12433078)	.84	09-19-07	–	10.4
14	Swamp Creek off Canfield Road, near Springdale (12433085)	1.09	09-25-07	–	11.5
15	Unnamed Tributary off Hidden Road, near Springdale (12433090)	.09	09-20-07	–	6.2
16	Unnamed Tributary at Hidden Road, near Springdale (12433094)	0	09-19-07	–	–
17	**Chamokane Creek near Springdale (12433100)**	0	09-18-07	-2.11	–
18	Unnamed Tributary at Fortymile Canyon Road, near Springdale (12433105)	0	09-25-07	–	–
19	Unnamed Tributary at Fortymile Canyon, near Springdale (12433110)	0	09-25-07	–	–
20	Unnamed Tributary off Reservation Road, near Ford (12433135)	.06	09-21-07	–	8.4
21	Rail Creek below Bartlett Creek, near Ford (12433145)	.18	09-25-07	–	8.7
22	Thomas Creek near Ford (12433155)	.32	09-27-07	–	9.7
23	Negro Creek near Ford (12433170)	.04	09-27-07	–	10.3
24	**Chamokane Creek at Ford-Wellpinit Road, near Ford (12433175)**	1.26	09-20-07	[1]0.66	10.3
25	Moses Creek near Ford (12433180)	.03	09-27-07	–	10.6
26	Galbraith Springs outflow near Ford (12433187)	4.18	10-11-07	–	11.5
27	Tribal hatchery outflow near Ford (12433190)	7.76	10-11-07	–	11.3
28	**Chamokane Creek below Falls near Long Lake (12433200)**	[2]28	09-20-07	[1]+19	–

[1]Value may not be representative of actual gain or loss along the mainstem of Chamokane Creek because discharge from tributary streams was measured closer to the headwaters of the tributaries than to their confluence with Chamokane Creek.

[2]Discharge calculated from gage height.

Table 6. High-flow investigation, Chamokane Creek, Spokane River basin, Stevens County, Washington, April 14–17, 2008.

[**Map No.** shown on plate 1. A series of discharge measurements were made April 14–17, 2008, on Chamokane Creek and some of its tributaries to study near-peak discharge (modifed from U.S. Geological Survey, 2008). The reach covered 30.7 miles. River mile 31.8 is the confluence of Little Chamokane Creek and Spokane River; river mile 32.5 is the confluence of Chamokane Creek and Spokane River. **Site name and location:** Site names in bold are located on the main stem of Chamokane Creek. Indented sites are tributary to the next listed site. **Abbreviations:** ft^3/s, cubic foot per second; C, degrees Celsius; –, no data]

Map No.	Site name and location	Measured discharge (ft^3/s)	Date	Net gain or loss (ft^3/s)	Water temperature (°C)
1	Middle Fork Chamokane Creek near Springdale (12433020)	206	04-14-08	–	3.7
2	South Fork Chamokane Creek near Springdale (12433030)	159	04-15-08	–	2.9
3	**Chamokane Creek below Forks near Springdale (12433035)**	333	04-15-08	-32.0	2.9
4	Unnamed Tributary at Rose Hill Road, near Springdale (12433040)	11.1	04-14-08	–	3.8
5	Unnamed Tributary at Springdale-Hunters Highway, near Springdale (12433043)	37.6	04-14-08	–	4.5
7	**Chamokane Creek at West Lyons Hill Road, near Springdale (12433055)**	425	04-15-08	+54.4	5.0
9	Unnamed Tributary Site 2 off Mickelson Road, near Springdale (12433062)	6.23	04-14-08	–	4.5
10	Unnamed Tributary above Drum Road, near Springdale (12433067)	3.66	04-17-08	–	7.6
11	**Chamokane Creek at East Lyons Hill Road, near Springdale (12433070)**	522	04-15-08	[1]+87.1	2.7
12	**Chamokane Creek above Swamp Creek, near Springdale (12433075)**	502	04-15-08	[2]-20.0	4.0
13	Swamp Creek at Cemetery Road, near Springdale (12433078)	2.87	04-14-08	–	12.6
14	Swamp Creek off Canfield Road, near Springdale (12433085)	2.10	04-15-08	–	10.5
15	Unnamed Tributary off Hidden Road, near Springdale (12433090)	1.44	04-14-08	–	–
16	Unnamed Tributary at Hidden Road, near Springdale (12433094)	1.46	04-14-08	–	–
17	**Chamokane Creek near Springdale (12433100)**	348	04-16-08	[3]-159	5.9
18	Unnamed Tributary at Fortymile Canyon Road, near Springdale (12433105)	6.50	04-14-08	–	–
19	Unnamed Tributary at Fortymile Canyon, near Springdale (12433110)	6.78	04-14-08	–	–
20	Unnamed Tributary off Reservation Road, near Ford (12433135)	1.09	04-15-08	–	4.5
21	Rail Creek below Bartlett Creek, near Ford (12433145)	15.9	04-14-08	–	4.9
22	Thomas Creek near Ford (12433155)	1.14	04-15-08	–	8.3
23	Negro Creek near Ford (12433170)	8.08	04-14-08	–	5.1
24	**Chamokane Creek at Ford-Wellpinit Road, near Ford (12433175)**	420	04-16-08	[1]+32.5	6.0
25	Moses Creek near Ford (12433180)	3.57	04-15-08	–	4.3
26	Galbraith Springs outflow near Ford (12433187)	7.23	04-17-08	–	12.6
27	Tribal hatchery outflow near Ford (12433190)	9.87	04-17-08	–	11.7
28	**Chamokane Creek below Falls, near Long Lake (12433200)**	422	04-16-08	-11.4	–

[1]Value may not be representative of actual gain or loss along the main stem of Chamokane Creek because discharge from tributary streams was measured closer to the headwaters of the tributaries than to their confluence with Chamokane Creek.

[2]Calculated difference may be less than measurement accuracy.

[3]Part of this apparent loss may be due to overall drop in flows from April 15 to April 16, 2008.

The second set of synoptic discharge measurements was completed between April 14 and 17, 2008 (table 6) to characterize high streamflow conditions. It was not possible to determine how close to the actual peak discharge these individual measurements were, but the timing of the measurements overlapped with the 2008 water year peak discharge (625 ft^3/s) for Chamokane Creek below Falls on April 15. Spring runoff flows can increase and decrease rapidly making it difficult to collect complete comparison data between sites when it is not possible to complete all measurements at the same time. This problem is clearly illustrated at site 12433055 (Chamokane Creek at West Lyons Hill Road) where two measurements were made one day apart during the high flow period. Measured discharge at site 12433055 was 425 ft^3/s on April 15, 2008 (table 6), but had decreased to 315 ft^3/s when a follow up measurement was made the next day. This decrease of 110 ft^3/s, just over 25 percent, is not unusual during a runoff event. The measurement results were supported by high water marks observed on April 16 that indicated the stream had already decreased about 2 ft from its recent peak.

The April 2008 high-flow measurements indicate that Chamokane Creek generally gained flow in its headwaters and along the length of Camas Valley until it achieved its greatest measured discharge (522 ft^3/s) at site 12433070 (Chamokane Creek at East Lyons Hill Road near Springdale) close to the eastern edge of Camas Valley. The creek then began losing flow steadily downstream toward the Walkers Prairie area. Measured discharge was only 348 ft^3/s at the gaging station (12433100). Farther downstream, discharge increased due to tributary input as the creek continued southward across Walkers Prairie. The most significant tributary contribution in this section was from Rail Creek where 15.9 ft^3/s was measured at site 12433145 (Rail Creek below Bartlett Creek near Ford). No significant difference in discharge was measured between the south end of Walkers Prairie at site 12433175 (Chamokane Creek at Ford-Wellpinit Road near Ford; 420 ft^3/s) and at Chamokane Creek below Falls (422 ft^3/s).

The final seepage run was done in late August 2008 using the same measurement locations (table 7) except site 12433187 (Galbraith Springs outflow near Ford) and site 12433190 (Tribal hatchery outflow near Ford), which were measured on September 2, 2008. This was an opportune time frame for this final set of seepage run measurements because the monthly mean discharge for August 2008 for Chamokane Creek below Falls was equal to the long term monthly mean of 27 ft^3/s at the same station for the period of record. Data from the 2008 seepage run showed similar low-flow trends to those determined in the initial 2007 seepage run. Conditions can differ substantially at low-flow from one year to another due to seasonal weather variations and annual flow magnitude. It should not be assumed that they are representative of other periods even though results of the 2007 and 2008 seepage runs follow each other closely. No flow (or little flow) was measured throughout the upper reaches of Chamokane Creek, including the headwaters and Camas Valley sections in 2007 and 2008. The only tributary in this section where any significant flow was measured was at site 12433067 (Unnamed Tributary above Drum Road near Springdale) where 0.18 ft^3/s was measured both years. Flows for site 12433075 (Chamokane Creek above Swamp Creek near Springdale) were nearly the same both years. Measured streamflow for Swamp Creek were slightly higher in 2008, but those small differences may be because the 2008 measurements were made about 1 month earlier in the year. No flow or minimal flow was measured in the Walkers Prairie area both years with no flow observed at Chamokane Creek near Springdale during both seepage runs. No flow was observed in the creek on July 29, 1 month prior to the 2008 seepage run at this site.

Flow becomes intermittent early in the low flow season at many reaches in the Walkers Prairie area and dry channel reaches have been observed as early as May 27 in 2009. Measured discharge at Chamokane Creek at Ford-Wellpinit Road (1243317) was 1.26 ft^3/s on September 20, 2007, and 1.65 ft^3/s on August 28, 2008. The most noteworthy characteristic of Chamokane Creek streamflow is that nearly all of the total flow measured at Chamokane Creek below Falls during the low flow time of year is provided by groundwater discharge, mostly from large springs and numerous seeps in the section downstream of Ford and from outflow from hatcheries which is a combination of water from wells and springs.

Table 7.   Seepage investigation, Chamokane Creek, Spokane River basin, Stevens County, Washington, August 25–September 2, 2008.

[**Map No.** shown on plate 1. A series of discharge measurements were made August 25–September 2, 2008, on Chamokane Creek and some of its tributaries to study gains and losses (modified from U.S. Geological Survey, 2008). The reach covered 30.7 miles. River mile 31.8 is the confluence of Little Chamokane Creek and Spokane River; river mile 32.5 is the confluence of Chamokane Creek and Spokane River. **Site name and location:** Site names in bold are located on the main stem of Chamokane Creek. Indented sites are tributary to the next listed site. **Abbreviations**: ft³/s, cubic foot per second; C, degrees Celsius; –, no data]

Map No.	Site name and location	Measured discharge (ft³/s)	Date	Gain or loss (ft³/s)	Water temperature (°C)
1	Middle Fork Chamokane Creek near Springdale (12433020)	0	08-25-08	–	15.7
2	South Fork Chamokane Creek near Springdale (12433030)	.08	08-25-08	–	13.7
3	**Chamokane Creek below Forks, near Springdale (12433035)**	0	08-25-08	–	14.6
4	Unnamed Tributary at Rose Hill Road, near Springdale (12433040)	0	08-25-08	–	–
5	Unnamed Tributary at Springdale-Hunters Highway, near Springdale (12433043)	0	08-25-08	–	–
6	Unnamed Tributary at Bowler Road, near Springdale (12433048)	0	08-26-08	–	12.4
7	**Chamokane Creek at West Lyons Hill Road, near Springdale (12433055)**	0	08-26-08	–	16.2
9	Unnamed Tributary Site 2 off Mickelson Road, near Springdale (12433062)	.02	08-25-08	–	8.5
10	Unnamed Tributary above Drum Road, near Springdale (12433067)	.18	08-26-08	–	13.4
11	**Chamokane Creek at East Lyons Hill Road, near Springdale (12433070)**	.04	08-26-08	[1]-0.16	19.6
12	**Chamokane Creek above Swamp Creek, near Springdale (12433075)**	1.00	08-29-08	+.96	13.1
13	Swamp Creek at Cemetery Road, near Springdale (12433078)	1.00	08-28-08	–	14.2
14	Swamp Creek off Canfield Road, near Springdale (12433085)	1.43	08-28-08	–	14.5
15	Unnamed Tributary off Hidden Road, near Springdale (12433090)	0	08-28-08	–	–
16	Unnamed Tributary at Hidden Road, near Springdale (12433094)	0	08-28-08	–	–
17	**Chamokane Creek near Springdale (12433100)**	0	08-28-08	-2.43	14.4
18	Unnamed Tributary at Fortymile Canyon Road, near Springdale (12433105)	.02	08-27-08	–	11.9
19	Unnamed Tributary at Fortymile Canyon, near Springdale (12433110)	0	08-27-08	–	–
20	Unnamed Tributary off Reservation Road, near Ford (12433135)	.05	08-27-08	–	13.7
21	Rail Creek below Bartlett Creek, near Ford (12433145)	.35	08-29-08	–	12.4
22	Thomas Creek near Ford (12433155)	.30	08-28-08	–	10.6
23	Negro Creek near Ford (12433170)	.02	08-29-08	–	13.9
24	**Chamokane Creek at Ford-Wellpinit Road, near Ford (12433175)**	1.65	08-28-08	[1]+.91	13.7
25	Moses Creek near Ford (12433180)	.04	08-28-08	–	12.7
26	Galbraith Springs outflow near Ford (12433187)	1.98	09-02-08	–	12.0
27	Tribal hatchery outflow near Ford (12433190)	7.95	09-02-08	–	12.8
28	**Chamokane Creek below Falls, near Long Lake (12433200)**	29.6	08-29-08	[1]+20.0	–

[1]Value may not be representative of actual gain or loss along the main stem of Chamokane Creek because discharge from tributary streams was measured closer to the headwaters of the tributaries than to their confluence with Chamokane Creek.

Interactions Between Groundwater and Surface Water

The data presented on the surface-water system indicates that there is considerable interaction between the near-surface hydrogeologic units and the surface water of the basin. Streamflow gains and losses along many reaches vary from month to month and from year to year. Exceptions to this were determined at the stream reaches with flow supported by perennial springs, most notably downstream of Ford where large springs discharge from the Upper outwash aquifer. Other spring-supported areas include Swamp Creek and Chamokane Creek between Ice Box Canyon and its confluence with Swamp Creek (Kessler, 2008).

During the high-flow measurements made for this investigation, gains in streamflow occurred throughout the Camas Valley with the largest high-flow measurement (522 ft³/s) made at the mouth of Ice Box Canyon after Chamokane Creek exits Camas Valley. From the mouth of Ice Box Canyon to the northern end of Walkers Prairie large streamflow losses were recorded indicating that Chamokane Creek loses flow directly to the Upper outwash aquifer in that reach. Modest gains occurred along Chamokane Creek through Walkers Prairie, apparently due to inputs from tributary streams rather than groundwater discharge to the creek. An overall small loss of flow was measured downstream of Ford to the gaging station downstream of Chamokane Falls indicating modest recharge to the Upper outwash aquifer in the lower end of the basin.

In contrast, under low-flow conditions, only two reaches along Chamokane Creek show any significant gains in flow and both are due to springs discharging from the Upper outwash aquifer. The first area is between the outlet of Ice Box Canyon and just upstream of the confluence of Chamokane and Swamp Creeks where gains of about 1 ft³/s were measured in each of the low-flow measurements in 2007 and 2008. The second area is downstream of Ford to near the gaging station at Chamokane Falls, where gains of about 20 ft³/s were measured during both low-flow measurements. The largest loss in flow during both low-flow measurements, slightly more than 2 ft³/s, was measured between Chamokane Creek just upstream of its confluence with Swamp Creek and the northeast end of Walkers Prairie.

Additional comparisons of gain/loss patterns for specific reaches between low-flow and high-flow is valuable and has important implications for groundwater/surface-water interaction. For example, a small loss was measured during low flow, but a large gain was measured during high flow in the reach upstream of the outlet of Ice Box Canyon. The reach between the outlet of Ice Box Canyon and the confluence of Chamokane and Swamp Creeks gained during low flow and lost during high flow. These examples illustrate changes in the direction of groundwater/surface water fluxes as a function of hydrologic conditions.

Land Use and Land Cover Change Analysis

A land use and land cover (LULC) change analysis was done to supplement the understanding of the Chamokane Creek basin groundwater and surface-water system. Changes in land use and land cover can result in changes in recharge to the groundwater system and changes in how water is used in the basin. The overall goal of the analysis was to document LULC types near the time of the adjudication (1979) and currently (2009), and compare LULC changes between those two periods. A combination of satellite imagery classification using geospatial software, inspection of historical areal photos, and field verification of current LULC classes was used for this analysis. The complete LULC analysis is presented in appendix A, including data acquisition, image classification, accuracy assessment, and limitations. LULC data will be incorporated into the GSFLOW model that will be completed during Phase 2 of this project. A summary of the LULC analysis detailed in appendix A is provided below.

The LULC change analysis was done using images from clear days, unobstructed by cloud cover, on October 11, 1987, and July 3, 2009. Although data at the time of adjudication would have been ideal for this analysis, high quality satellite images were not available until October 1987.

Seven LULC classes were identified in the classification process.

Evergreen forest – Areas dominated by evergreen trees greater than 5 m tall.

Open forest – Areas of open, low-density evergreen trees that are greater than 5 m tall. These areas may be naturally open ponderosa pine forests or low-density forests resulting from harvesting activities.

Shrub – Areas dominated by shrubs less than 5 m tall. These areas include true shrubs and young trees in an early successional stage.

Grassland – Areas covered by grasses and other herbaceous vegetation. These areas are not subject to intensive management activities but may be used for grazing.

Agriculture – Land that is used for the production of crops and is being actively tilled. Also includes pastures planted for livestock grazing.

Developed/sparsely vegetated – Areas where there is little vegetation due to the presence of constructed materials, impervious surfaces, bare/barren land, or clearcuts.

Water – Areas of open water.

The area distribution for LULC classes in 1987 and 2009 is shown in figure 13. Forest cover is the dominant land cover type in the Chamokane Creek basin in 1987 and 2009. Between 1987 and 2009, however, evergreen forest cover decreased by nearly 11,000 acres, or 14.5 percent of the original forest cover. Much of this decrease was a result of a change in classification of 9,800 acres of evergreen forest to open forest. Additionally, 5,300 acres of evergreen forest became shrub, 2,300 acres became grassland and 1,300 acres became developed/sparsely vegetated. Major changes in land cover *to* the evergreen forest category include 1,800 acres of grassland, 4,900 acres of shrub, and 740 acres of open forest. Therefore, the net changes of evergreen forest to shrub and evergreen forest to grassland were relatively small (less than about 500 acres).

Open forest cover increased from 6.97 to 17.4 percent of the total basin area (an increase of more than 12,000 acres). As mentioned previously, this increase is predominantly due to a change in classification of about 9,800 acres of evergreen forest to open forest. Other major changes include about 1,800 acres of grassland, 1,600 acres of shrub, and 1,800 acres of agriculture becoming open forest in 2009. About 1,800 acres of open forest changed in classification to grassland so the net change between open forest and grassland was minor. About 740 acres of open forest changed to evergreen forest.

Chamokane Creek basin currently (2009) is an area dominated by forests with some pasture and agricultural lands. Development is still relatively sparse. Loss in forest cover represents the largest change in land cover in the basin between 1987 and 2009. This appears to be mostly due to forestry activities, especially in the northern part of the basin. Some of the loss in forest cover north of Ford may have been due to a 5,300-acre fire (less than half of which was originally in forest cover) that occurred in 1991. Since 1987, more than 18,000 acres of evergreen forest have been logged and are at various stages of regrowth.

Recently, 1,300 of these acres were harvested, falling under the classification of "developed/sparsely vegetated." Between 1987 and 2009, more than 7,000 acres of shrub, grassland and open forest changed in classification to evergreen forest, indicating previously logged areas that have now regenerated.

Much of the increase in the open forest classification from 1987 to 2009 also is due to harvesting practices. Areas likely are being converted from evergreen forest to low-density, open forests from logging activities. Although to a lesser extent, changes from evergreen forest to open forest also may be due to development activities, especially between the towns of Ford and Springdale. Development in the basin is at such a small scale relative to the pixel size of the satellite sensors (30 m^2) that some development in this heavily forested area may be picked up only as open forest rather than developed/sparsely vegetated.

Changes in shrub cover mainly occurred on lands where forestry activities took place. Changes from shrub cover, specifically of young evergreen trees, to forest cover likely are a result of regeneration, although changes from forest cover to shrub are due to recent logging activities, where regeneration is still ongoing.

Changes that involve deciduous shrub cover, grasslands, and agricultural lands are difficult to analyze because the 1987 image was taken in autumn and the 2009 image was taken in summer. The difference in seasons of the two images may influence the LULC classifications, with deciduous plants looking vastly different between the summer and autumn, herbaceous plants dying back at the end of the growing season, and crops drying and being harvested at various points in time. Furthermore, although it appears that a substantial decrease in the amount of agricultural lands and an increase in the amount of grasslands in the basin occurred, further investigation is necessary to make this determination. Pastureland also may have been classified as agriculture in some areas and as grassland in other areas. Although agriculture may have decreased in the basin, it is unlikely to have decreased to the extent shown by this analysis.

This analysis highlighted major changes that occurred in the Chamokane Creek basin between 1987 and 2009, specifically regarding evergreen forest cover. The analysis also will provide more specific LULC data for the GSFLOW model compared to the generalized LULC products that currently are available. Additional studies would be needed to answer questions regarding changes in agriculture and specific crop types as well as changes in developed land area.

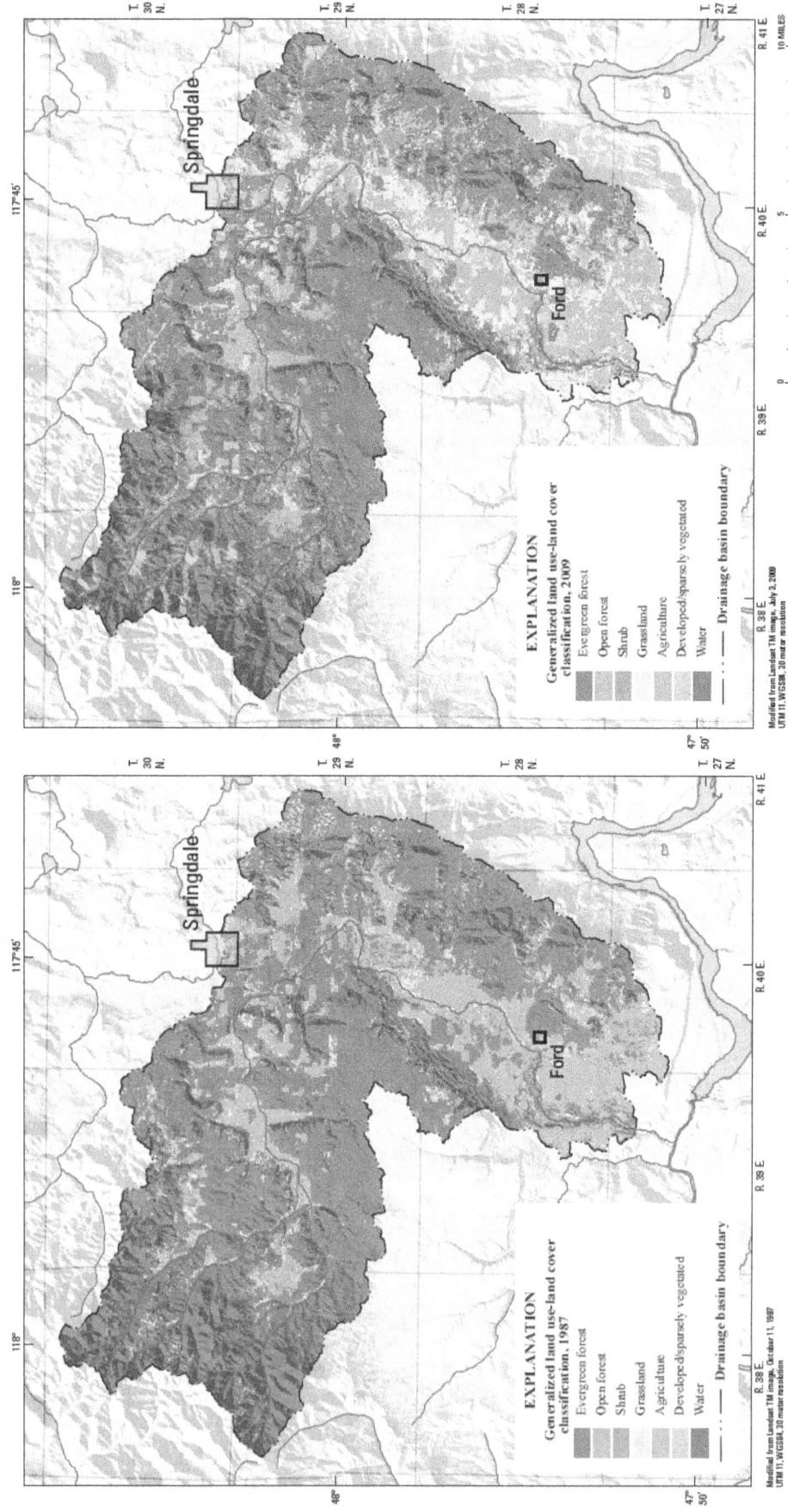

Figure 13.   Generalized land use and land cover classifications, Chamokane Creek basin, Stevens County, Washington, 1987 and 2009.

Groundwater Pumpage and Use

Groundwater pumpage was estimated so water use within the basin could be estimated near the time of adjudication through present (2009) for permit exempt and non-exempt uses of groundwater. Annual groundwater pumpage estimates for 1980 through 2007 in the Chamokane Creek basin are shown in table 8.

The major uses of water in the Chamokane Creek basin are for domestic purposes (single-family drinking and household use, lawns, and small gardens), public water supply, fish-hatchery operations, irrigation, and commercial and industrial uses. Some surface water may be withdrawn from Chamokane Creek for these purposes, but the primary source of water is groundwater. Based on water rights on file with the State of Washington and reported by the Lower Spokane Basin Watershed Planning website, less than 100,000 gal/yr of water are removed from the creek (Tetra Tech/KLM, 2007, accessed March 23, 2009, at http://www.spokanecounty.org/wqmp/project54/ASP/P2L1TechAssmnt_index.asp).

Annual groundwater pumpage in the Chamokane Creek basin was estimated and compared from 1980 through 2007 for five major categories: self-supplied domestic, public water supply, aquaculture, irrigation, and commercial/industrial (table 8). Self-supplied domestic and public-supply estimates were based on U.S. Census Bureau population data and a per-person water use estimate derived from data presented in a report on the water resources of the Colville River Watershed (Kahle and others, 2003). U.S. Census Bureau population data, in the form of a geographic information system (GIS) data layer, were obtained from the Washington State Office of Financial Management (accessed August 2007 at http://www.ofm.wa.gov/pop/geographic/00tiger.asp). The data layer contained the distribution of population by census block, the smallest area for which the Census Bureau tabulates census data. Water use of 210 gal/d per person was computed from population and estimated water-use data compiled by the Water-Resource Inventory Area (WRIA) 59 Colville River Watershed Planning team (Kahle and others, 2003). The population and per-person water use data were combined to estimate domestic and public-supply water use in the study area. Pumpage estimates for the other uses were compiled from Spokane Tribal water managers, public-water system managers and records, agencies of the State of Washington (Departments of Health, Ecology, Fish and Wildlife, and Agriculture), and from private citizens.

Annual groundwater pumpage values from 1980 through 2007 for the study area range from 21.1 to 28.9 Mgal/yr for domestic wells and 0.38 to 23.7 Mgal/yr for public supply wells (table 8). A sharp increase in public-supply pumpage (from 0.38 Mgal in 1987 to 9.4 Mgal in 1988) reflects the addition of several public supply systems in the basin.

Pumpage estimates for years after the 2000 census are based on Census Bureau interdecadal population estimates.

Population distribution during 2000 in the study area indicates that the highest concentration of people is in the areas west and south of Springdale, Wash. (fig. 14). Self-supplied domestic well pumpage during 2000 reflects the population distribution with the highest annual pumpage west and south of Springdale (fig. 15). Service areas for the public-supply wells were considered to be the quarter-quarter section in the legal description for the well. The distribution of public-supply pumpage also is presented in figure 15.

Groundwater pumpage for the hatcheries is presented in table 8. The combined total of water pumped for the two hatcheries for aquaculture for 2007 was about 1.15 billion gallons. Ground-water pumpage by the hatcheries increased by about a factor of 5 from 1997 to 2007 as the Tribal hatchery increased usage in 2003 and with the drilling of a production well and subsequent use of groundwater at the WDFW hatchery in 2005. No pre-adjudication pumpage estimates for aquaculture were computed because the Tribal hatchery and the WDFW hatchery relied on spring water until 1990 and 2005, respectively.

Little commercial or industrial activity currently (2009) occurs in the study area. Excluding the water used by the Ford Trading Post, which is included in the public-supply estimate, the only other commercial/industrial user is the Dawn Mining Company millsite at Ford, Wash. From 1970 to 1982, the mill used about 105 Mgal of water per year for ore processing. From 1983 through 1991, mining and milling operations were suspended and an unknown, but small, amount of water was used. The mill was re-opened in 1992 to process sludge from a water-treatment plant at the mine site and water use was about 0.34 Mgal/yr. Sludge processing continued intermittently until 2001. From 2001 through 2007, continuous maintenance at the mill used about 26.3 Mgal/yr. Some return flow to Chamokane Creek resulted from the maintenance operations, but the amount is unknown (Robert Nelson, Dawn Mining Company, oral commun., 2010).

Of about 4,400 acres of land within the study area classified as agricultural land, only about 160 acres was irrigated with groundwater in 2007. In 1987, the first year when reliable agricultural acreage was calculated, the area irrigated was about 150 acres. Water use by crop type was obtained from the AgriMet station maintained by the Bureau of Reclamation in the study area (Bureau of Reclamation, AgriMet, accessed October 14, 2009, at http://www.usbr.gov/pn/agrimet/wa_charts.html). The area and location of each crop type were obtained from GIS data layers that were derived from satellite imagery of the study area (see Land use and land cover change analysis and appendix A). The amount of water used by each crop type and the acreage of each crop type were combined to compute agricultural water use.

Table 8. Annual groundwater pumpage for Chamokane Creek basin, Stevens County, Washington.

[Pumpage is in millions of gallons; E, estimated value; –, data not available]

	1980	1981	1982	1983	1984	1985	1986	1987	1988	1989	1990	1991	1992	1993	Average annual pumpage
Domestic	21.1	21.2	21.4	21.5	21.7	21.6	21.2	21.1	20.7	20.4	20.2	20.5	21.4	22.0	24.0
Public supply	0.38	0.38	0.38	0.38	0.38	0.38	0.38	0.38	9.4	9.8	11.0	11.6	12.1	12.9	11.6
Aquaculture	105	105	105	–	–	–	–	–	–	–	191	192	192	192	416
Commercial/Industrial	–	–	–	–	–	–	–	–	–	–	–	–	0.34	0.34	26
Agriculture	98E	98E	98E	98E	98E	98E	98E	97.9	98.1	98.3	98.5	98.7	98.9	99.1	100
Total annual pumpage	224	225	225	120	120	120	120	119	128	128	321	323	325	326	420

	1994	1995	1996	1997	1998	1999	2000	2001	2002	2003	2004	2005	2006	2007
Domestic	23.1	24.2	25.2	26.3	26.6	27.0	28.4	28.2	27.9	27.7	27.4	27.5	28.2	28.9
Public supply	13.5	14.1	14.9	15.5	16.1	16.8	17.6	18.3	19.1	19.9	20.9	21.7	22.7	23.7
Aquaculture	192	192	192	220	250	250	250	250	250	630	885	956	1,060	1,150
Commercial/Industrial	0.34	0.34	0.34	0.34	0.34	0.34	0.34	26.3	26.3	26.3	26.3	26.3	26.3	26.3
Agriculture	99.3	99.5	99.7	99.9	100	100	100	101	101	102	102	102	103	103
Total annual pumpage	328	330	332	362	393	394	396	424	424	806	1,060	1,130	1,240	1,330

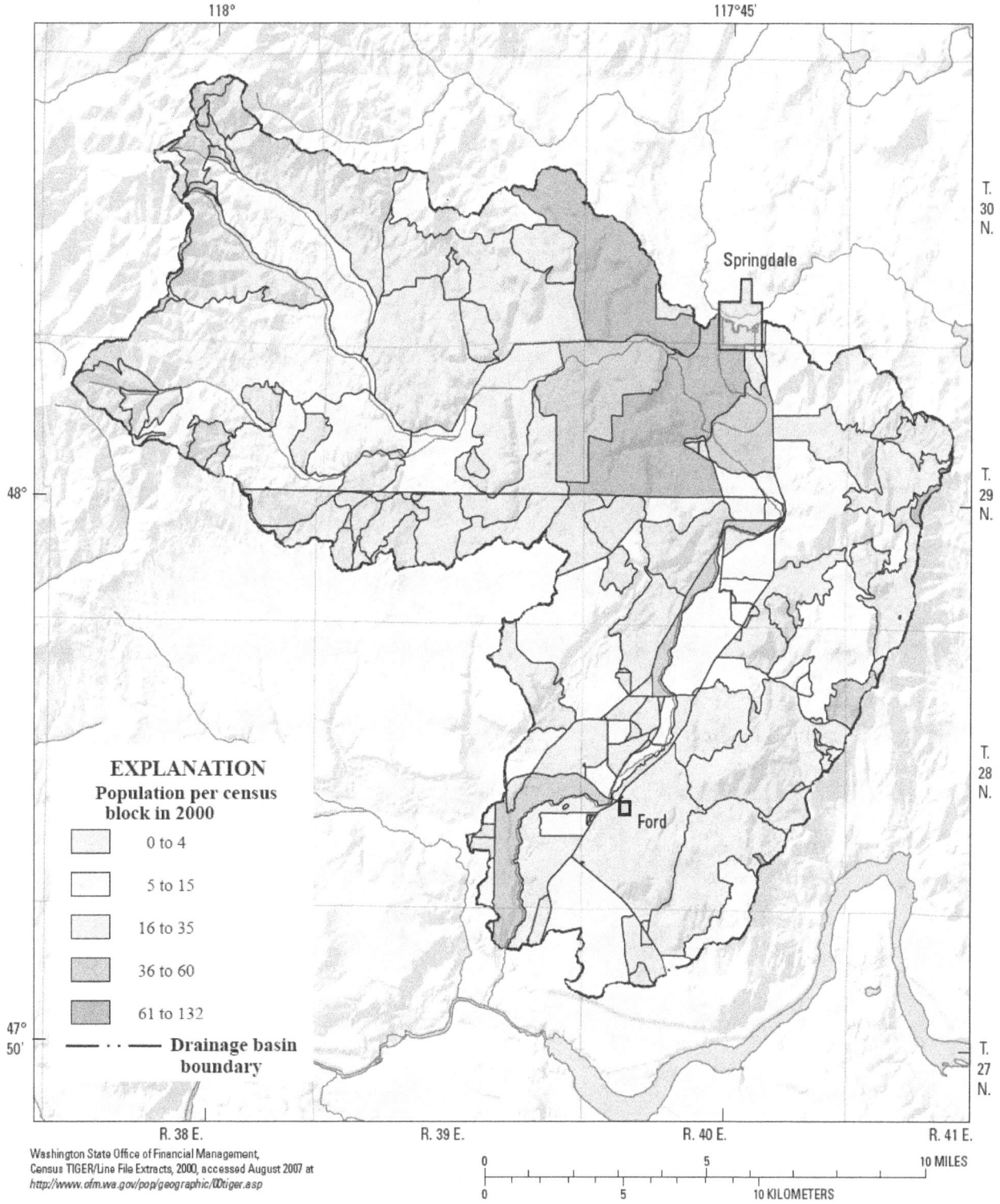

Figure 14.   Distribution of Census blocks and 2000 population, Chamokane Creek basin, Stevens County, Washington. Census blocks were obtained from Washington State Office of Financial Management, Census TIGER/Line File Extracts, 2000, accessed August 2007 at http://www.ofm.wa.gov/pop/geographic/00tiger.asp.

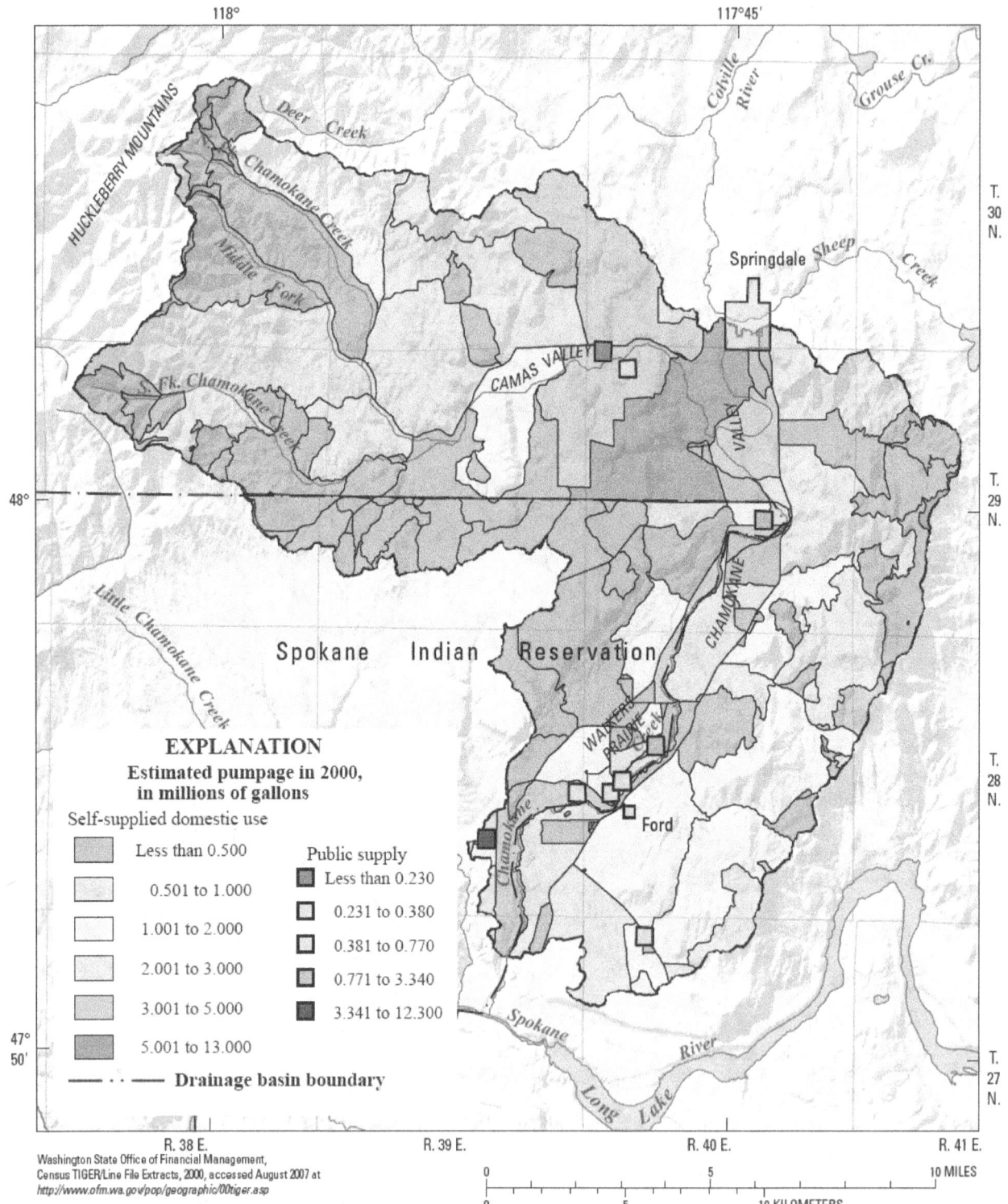

Figure 15. Distribution of estimated pumpage in 2000 for self-supplied domestic use and public supply, Chamokane Creek basin, Stevens County, Washington.

In 1987, about 97.9 Mgal of groundwater was pumped to irrigate crops in the study area. In 2007, about 103 Mgal of groundwater was pumped. Estimates of agricultural land were not determined for years between 1987 and 2007, however, assuming that the amount of irrigated agricultural land from 1987 to 2007 increased uniformly from 150 acres (the 1987 value) to 160 acres (the 2007 value), estimates of pumpage for agricultural use can be computed using the same rate of change, about 5 percent per year. Pumpage from 1987 to 2007 pumpage then was estimated to increase by about 0.2 Mgal/yr. Due to a lack of agricultural acrage data prior to 1987, an estimate of 98 Mgal/yr was used for 1980–86 (table 8).

Basin Water Budget

On a long-term basis, a hydrologic system is usually in a state of dynamic equilibrium; that is, inflow to the system is equal to outflow from the system and there is little or no change in the quantity of water stored within the system. Based on long-term groundwater levels shown in figure 11, this appears to be the case for the Chamokane Creek basin where long-term mining or mounding of the aquifer system is not apparent. An estimated water budget, or distribution of precipitation, for a typical year in the Chamokane Creek basin includes estimates of component values, and illustrates the fate of precipitation (inflow) by approximating the distribution of water in the hydrologic system of the basin: precipitation (inflow) and evapotranspiration, streamflow, and groundwater discharge (outflow). It is assumed that, in the long term, inflow to the basin equals outflow and little or no change is expected in the amount of water stored within the basin. This relation is shown as:

$$\begin{aligned} \text{Precipitation} = {}& \text{Evapotranspiration} \\ &+ \text{Streamflow at outlet} \\ &+ \text{Groundwater discharge at outlet; and} \\ &\quad \text{for the study area :} \end{aligned} \tag{4}$$

$$19.6 \text{ in.} = 14.9 \text{ in.} + 4.7 \text{ in.} + 0 \text{ in.} \tag{5}$$

Equation 4 shows the water-budget components and equation 5 shows the estimated value for each component, in inches, derived for the study area.

A statistical-topographic model for mapping climatological precipitation over mountainous terrain, PRISM (Daly and others, 1994), was used to derive an area-weighted average precipitation of 19.6 in. for the Chamokane Creek basin. The distribution of average annual precipitation (1971–2000) for the basin, contoured using data from NOAA weather stations and USDA-Natural Resource Conservation Service snow-measurement stations, is shown in figure 2. Averaging the ranges of precipitation over the basin yielded the area-weighted average of 19.6 in. Discharge from Chamokane Creek near the outlet of the basin (4.7 in.) was based on the long-term average flow (62.5 ft³/s) at gaging station 12433200 for the 28 years when a complete record was available (1972–78 and 1988–2008). Groundwater discharge near the outlet of the basin is assumed to be zero. The value for evapotranspiration (14.9 in.) is a residual; that is, it represents the quantity that remains after Chamokane Creek discharge is subtracted from precipitation.

The predominant fate of precipitation in the basin (76 percent) is loss from the basin through evapotranspiration, a combination of evaporation from open bodies of water, evaporation from soil surfaces, and transpiration from the soil by plants. Evapotranspiration commonly accounts for the greatest loss from basins with similar hydrologic conditions. For comparison, evapotranspiration losses were 78 percent of precipitation in the Colville River basin (Ely and Kahle, 2004).

Streamflow leaving the basin, as measured downstream of Chamokane Falls, is 24 percent of precipitation. Total groundwater use for 2007, is an estimated 1,330 Mgal/yr (table 8). Of that total, 1,150 Mgal/yr is pumped for the fish hatcheries, and nearly all of that gets discharged to Chamokane Creek and 'counted' as streamflow past the gage. Therefore, actual groundwater use in the basin (2007) is approximately 180 Mgal/yr, or only about .3 percent of total precipitation. This simple comparison indicates that actual groundwater use is relatively small when compared to total precipitation.

Data Needs

Additional information about the thickness of the Lower aquifer is needed to understand better the deepest parts of the groundwater system in the Chamokane Creek basin. The thickness of the Lower aquifer could be better determined by drilling into underlying basalt or older bedrock. Deep drilling at several locations along the axis of the Chamokane Valley from the Swamp Creek area to near Ford would provide these two important pieces of information.

Independent data on return flows or consumptive use of pumpage would be helpful to gain a more complete understanding of water use within the basin. Although the GSFLOW model being used in Phase 2 of this study may provide some insights, independent data would provide a more complete understanding of water use. The greatest pumpage in the basin is associated with activities such as aquaculture and in the past, industry, that tend to have significant return flows. Data on domestic consumptive use or septic returns also would be helpful to better quantify timing and magnitude of effects on streamflow.

A water budget for the groundwater system is more difficult to estimate than the basin water budget because of limited knowledge of component values. During Phase 2 of this study, the GSFLOW model will be used to provide estimates of recharge to the groundwater system as well as a comprehensive water budget. The calibrated model will provide a more refined depiction of the groundwater and surface-water flow system where current observational data are lacking.

Summary

Chamokane Creek basin is a 179 mi^2 area that borders and partially overlaps the Spokane Indian Reservation in southern Stevens County in northeastern Washington State. Aquifers in the Chamokane Creek basin are part of a sequence of glaciofluvial and glaciolacustrine sediment that may reach a total thickness of about 600 ft. In 1979, most of the water rights in the Chamokane Creek basin were adjudicated by the United States District Court requiring regulation in favor of the Spokane Tribe of Indian's senior water right. A court-appointed Water Master regulates junior water rights when the mean daily 7-day low flow becomes less than 24 ft^3/s (27 ft^3/s for rights issued after December 1988) at Chamokane Falls, as recorded at U.S. Geological Survey (USGS) streamflow-gaging station 12433200; regulation has been necessary in 3 recent years (2001, 2005, and 2008). Additionally, the non-Reservation areas of the basin are closed to additional groundwater or surface-water appropriations, with the exception of permit exempt uses of groundwater.

Data from 158 wells were used to characterize the hydrogeologic framework and analyze the direction of groundwater movement in the Chamokane Creek basin. Water levels were measured in wells during three study periods: autumn 2007, spring 2008, and late summer 2008. Additionally, a monthly water-level network of 25 wells was monitored from March 2008 through December 2009. Six wells in the monthly network were instrumented with transducers for the collection of hourly water-level measurements.

Six hydrogeologic units described in this report include the Upper outwash aquifer, the Landslide unit, the Valley confining unit, the Lower aquifer, the Basalt unit and the Bedrock unit. The Upper outwash aquifer is an unconfined aquifer that occurs along the valley floors of the study area. It consists of sand, gravel, cobbles, and boulders, with minor silt and (or) clay interbeds in places. Thickness of the aquifer ranges from less than 50 ft along the margins of the unit to more than 150 ft where the unit is comprised of glacial terraces. The Landslide unit is composed of poorly sorted deposits of broken basalt and sedimentary interbeds along the basalt bluffs bounding Walkers Prairie. The Valley

confining unit is a mostly low-permeability unit consisting of glaciolacustrine silt and clay that occurs at depth throughout the valley bottoms of the study area and extends northward into the Colville Valley. The thickness of the Valley confining unit commonly is 150–300 ft. The Lower aquifer is a confined aquifer consisting of sand and gravel that occurs at depth below the Valley confining unit; it too extends northward into the Colville Valley. Thickness of the unit is not well known throughout its extent, but thicknesses of two wells that fully penetrated the unit were 125 and 138 ft. The Basalt unit is composed of Columbia River Basalt and sedimentary interbeds. Water is contained in cracks and fractures and from zones between lava flows. The Bedrock unit includes rocks older than the Columbia River Basalt and commonly includes granite and quartzite with small and often unreliable yields. Median horizontal hydraulic conductivity values for the Upper outwash aquifer, Valley confining unit, Lower aquifer, and Basalt unit were estimated to be 540, 10, 19, and 3.7 ft/d, respectively.

Horizontal groundwater flow in the Upper outwash aquifer moves from the topographically high tributary-basin areas toward the topographically lower valley floors. Water-level altitudes in the Upper outwash aquifer range from 2,150 ft in the Camas Valley to 1,760 ft near Ford. The general distribution of horizontal gradients was about 13–50 ft/mi in the Camas Valley, about 80 ft/mi where Chamokane Creek exits Icebox Canyon to near its confluence with Swamp Creek, 20–30 ft/mi from south of Springdale through the Swamp Creek area, and 12–16 ft/mi along Walkers Prairie. The smallest gradient in the Upper outwash aquifer, about 12 ft/mi, was along Walkers Prairie.

Horizontal groundwater flow in the Lower aquifer is south to southwest from near Springdale to south of Ford. In the Camas Valley, horizontal groundwater flow is east to near the end of the valley where flow likely discharges into overlying sediments and Chamokane Creek near the end of the valley at the head of Icebox Canyon. Along the Chamokane Valley floor, water-level altitudes within the Lower aquifer range from 1,885 ft near Swamp Creek to 1,600 ft near the lower end of the basin. Horizontal gradients are about 20 ft/mi along Walkers Prairie, but become much greater and range from 80 to 200 ft/mi from near Ford to the southern extent of the Lower aquifer. In Camas Valley, water-level altitudes within the Lower aquifer range from about 2,150 to less than 2,050 ft. The horizontal gradient in Camas Valley is about 100 ft/mi.

Paired hydrographs for closely spaced wells completed in the Upper outwash aquifer and the Lower aquifer indicate a nearly identical timing of the seasonal rise and falls in water levels with similar, but slightly greater magnitude in the fluctuations in the Upper outwash aquifer. The overall similarity of fluctuations in water levels indicates that these systems may be fairly well connected.

Three sets of synoptic discharge measurements were made at 28 sites along Chamokane Creek and its tributaries during this study to identify gaining and losing reaches during high- and low-flow conditions. Two sets of low-flow measurements were made at these sites in late September-early October 2007 and in August 2008. One set of high-flow measurements was made in mid-April 2008. During the low-flow measurements many sites were at or near zero flow. Exceptions to this include stream sections supported by spring flow, most notably downstream of Ford where large springs discharge from the Upper outwash aquifer. During the high-flow measurements, gains in streamflow occurred throughout the Camas Valley with the largest high-flow measurement (522 ft^3/s) made at the mouth of Ice Box Canyon. Downstream of Camas Valley, large streamflow losses were recorded that indicate that Chamokane Creek loses flow directly to the Upper outwash aquifer near the north end of Walkers Prairie.

A land use and land cover change analysis indicates that Chamokane Creek basin currently (2009) is an area dominated by forests with some pasture and agricultural lands. Development is relatively sparse. Loss in forest cover represents the largest change in land cover in the basin between 1987 and 2009. This appears to be mostly due to forestry activities, especially in the northern part of the basin. Since 1987, more than 18,000 acres of evergreen forest have been logged and are at various stages of regrowth.

Estimated average annual total groundwater pumpage in the basin increased from 224 Mgal/yr in 1980 to 1,330 Mgal/yr in 2007. In 2007, the largest withdrawals were to supply two fish hatcheries, with a combined total annual pumpage of about 1,150 Mgal. Annual groundwater pumpage values from 1980 through 2007 for the study area range from 21.1 to 28.9 Mgal/yr for domestic wells and 0.38 to 23.7 Mgal/yr for public supply.

An approximate water budget, or distribution of precipitation, for a typical year in the Chamokane Creek basin shows that 19.6 in. of precipitation are balanced by 4.7 in. of streamflow discharge from the basin, and 14.9 in. of evapotranspiration.

Acknowledgments

The authors of this report gratefully acknowledge the landowners who shared their knowledge and concerns about water-resources in the Chamokane Creek basin and allowed access to their property for data collection. Without their consent, it would have been impossible to collect most of the data required for this study. Steven Andrews, former Spokane Tribe Utilities manager, provided information concerning tribal public supply wells. Lam Chan, GIS Manager for the Spokane Tribe, provided digital data sets. Brian Crossley, Spokane Tribe Natural Resources, responded to numerous inquiries for data, references, and contact information pertaining to water-resources on the Spokane Reservation. Charlie Kessler, Stevens County Conservation District, provided insights on the surface-water system of the basin as well as detailed information collected as part of his Chamokane Creek Watershed Management work. Eugene Kiver, Eastern Washington University (retired), loaned original field maps of surficial geology for the Ford and Tum Tum 7 ½-minute quadrangles. Miles Logsdon, University of Washington, provided guidance and technical support on the land use classification and change analysis process. James Lylera, Chamokane Creek Water Master, provided long-term water-level data and water-use information for the basin. William Matt, Sr., Spokane Tribe Natural Resources, provided assistance in locating wells on the Reservation. Robert Nelson, Dawn Mining Company, provided water-use data for the Ford mill. Tim Peone and Ace Trump provided water-use information for the Tribal and Washington Department of Fish and Wildlife fish hatcheries, respectively. Donna Smith, Bureau of Indian Affairs, provided information on wells and population estimates for the Reservation.

References Cited

Allen, J.E., and Burns, Marjorie, 1986, Cataclysms on the Columbia: Portland, Oregon, Timber Press, Inc., 213 p.

Atwater, B.F., 1986, Pleistocene glacial-lake deposits of the Sanpoil River Valley, northeastern Washington: U.S. Geological Survey Bulletin 1661, 39 p.

Bear, Jacob, 1979, Hydraulics of groundwater: New York, McGraw-Hill, 569 p.

Buchanan, J.P., Wozniewicz, J.V., and Lambeth, R.H., 1988, Hydrogeology of the Chamokane Valley aquifer system: Upper Columbia United Tribes Fisheries Center, Eastern Washington University, Fisheries Technical Report No. 20, 69 p.

Bureau of Reclamation, 2009, AgriMet, The Pacific Northwest Cooperative Agricultural Weather Network: Bureau of Reclamation website accessed October 14, 2009, at http://www.usbr.gov/pn/agrimet/wa_charts.html.

Carnahan, B., Luther, H.A., and Wilkes, J.O., 1969, Applied numerical methods: New York, John Wiley and Sons, Inc., 604 p.

Carrara, P.E., Kiver, E.P., and Stradling, D.F., 1995, Surficial geologic map of the Chewelah 30' × 60' quadrangle, Washington and Idaho: U.S. Geological Survey Miscellaneous Investigations Series Map I-2472, 1 sheet, scale 1:100,000.

Carrara, P.E., Kiver, E.P., and Stradling, D.F., 1996, The southern limit of Cordilleran ice in the Colville and Pend Oreille valleys of northeastern Washington during the late Wisconsin glaciation: Canadian Journal of Earth Sciences, v. 33, no. 5, p. 769–778.

Daly, Chris, Neilson, R.P., and Phillips, D.L., 1994, A statistical-topographic model for mapping climatological precipitation over mountainous terrain: Journal of Applied Meteorology, v. 33, p. 140-158.

Drost, B.W., comp., 2005, Quality-assurance plan for ground-water activities, U.S. Geological Survey, Washington Water Science Center: U.S. Geological Survey Open-File Report 20051126, 27 p. (Available at http://pubs.usgs.gov/of/2005/1126/.)

Ely, D.M., and Kahle, S.C., 2004, Conceptual model and numerical simulation of the ground-water flow system in the unconsolidated deposits of the Colville River Watershed, Stevens County, Washington: U.S. Geological Survey Scientific Investigations Report 2004-5237, 72 p.

Embrey, S.S., Hansen, A.J., and Cline, D.R., 1997, Ground-water resources of three areas on the Spokane and Kalispel Indian Reservations, northeastern Washington: U.S. Geological Survey Water-Resources Investigations Report 94-4235, 67 p., 1 pl.

Ferris, J.G., Knowles, D.B., Brown, R.H., and Stallman, R.W., 1962, Theory of aquifer tests: U.S. Geological Survey Water-Supply Paper 1536-E, 174 p.

Flint, R.F., 1936, Stratified drift and deglaciation of eastern Washington: Geological Society of America Bulletin, v. 47, p. 1850-1884.

Freeze, R.A., and Cherry, J.A., 1979, Groundwater: Englewood Cliffs, N.J., Prentice-Hall, 604 p.

Golder Associates, Inc., 2008, Final report, conceptual site models for Martha Boardman/Kokanee Meadows and Ford/Newhouse Lane Water Systems: Coeur d'Alene, Idaho, prepared for Indian Health Service, Spokane, Wash., May 14, 2008, variously paginated.

Google™Earth, 2010, Satellite imagery, maps, and terrain: Google Earth website, accessed November 12, 2007, at http://earth.google.com/index.html.

Güler, Mustafa, Yomralioğlu Tahsin, and Reis, Selçuk 2007, Using landsat data to determine land use/land cover changes in Samsun, Turkey: Environmental Monitoring and Assessment, v. 127, no. 1–3, p. 113.

Howard, D.J., 1990, Geomorphology of Chamokane Creek below Ford, Washington: Cheney, Eastern Washington University, Master of Science thesis, 114 p.

Howard, D.J., Buchanan, J.P., and Stone, R.A., 1989, Geomorphology of Chamokane Creek below Ford, Washington: Upper Columbia United Tribes Fisheries Center, Eastern Washington University. Fisheries Technical Report No. 24, 112 p.

Hutchinson, M.F., 1989, A new method for gridding elevation and streamlining data with automated removal of pits: Journal of Hydrology, v. 106, p. 211-232.

Jensen, M.E., Burman, R.D., and Allen, R.G., eds., 1990, Evapotranspiration and irrigation water requirements: New York, ASCE Manuals and Reports on Engineering Practice No. 70, 332 p.

Kahle, S.C., Longpré, C.I., Smith, R.R., Sumioka, S.S., Watkins, A.M., and Kresch, D.L., 2003, Water resources of the ground-water system in the unconsolidated deposits of the Colville River watershed, Stevens County, Washington: U.S. Geological Survey Water-Resources Investigations Report 03-4128, 76 p.

King, J.M., Palmer, S.P., and Buchanan, J.P., 1996, Report of geophysical seismic reflection surveys conducted for the Spokane Tribe of Indians within an area located in the vicinity of the town of Ford, Washington: Lacey, Wash., SeisPulse Development Corporation, [variously paged].

Kessler, C., 2000a, Chamokane Creek Watershed Management Plan: Colville, Wash., Stevens County Conservation District, 121 p.

Kessler, C., 2000b, Chamokane Creek Watershed Water Quality Summary Report: Colville, Wash., Stevens County Conservation District, 31 p.

Kessler, C., 2008, Chamokane Creek Watershed Needs Assessment: Colville, Wash., Stevens County Conservation District, 68 p.

Kiver, E.P., and Stradling, D.F., 1982, Quaternary geology of the Spokane area, in Roberts, S., and Fountain, D., eds., 1980 Field Conference Guidebook: Spokane, Wash., Tobacco Root Geological Society, p. 26-44.

Kiver, E.P., Stradling, D.F., and Moody, U.L., 1989, Glacial and multiple flood history of the northern borderlands—Trip B, in Joseph, N.L., and others, eds., Geologic guidebook for Washington and adjacent areas: Washington Division of Geology and Earth Resources Information Circular 86, p. 321-335.

Lasmanis, R., 1991, The Geology of Washington: Rocks and Minerals, v. 66, no. 4, p. 262-277.

Lillesand, T. M., Kiefer, R.W., and W. Chipman, J.W., 2008, Remote sensing and image interpretation: Hoboken, N.J., John Wiley & Sons, 736 p.

Lukas, M.J., 1981, Hydrogeology study, groundwater potential for domestic water wells on the Spokane Indian Reservation, Washington: Portland, Oreg., United States Department of Health and Human Services, Public Health Service, Indian Health Service Portland Area Office, 67 p.

Markstrom, S.L., Niswonger, R.G., Regan, R.S., Prudic, D.E., and Barlow, P.M., 2008, GSFLOW-Coupled Ground-water and Surface-water FLOW model based on the integration of the Precipitation-Runoff Modeling System (PRMS) and the Modular Ground-Water Flow Model (MODFLOW-2005): U.S. Geological Survey Techniques and Methods 6-D1, 240 p., accessed March 23, 2010, at http://water.usgs.gov/nrp/gwsoftware/gsflow/gsflow.html.

Matt, V.J., 1994, Hydrology and hydrogeology of the Spokane Indian Reservation, northeastern Washington State: Cheney, Eastern Washington University, Master of Science thesis, 209 p.

Matt, V.J., and Buchanan, J.P., 1993a, Aquifer systems on the Spokane Indian Reservation: Upper Columbia United Tribes Fisheries Center, Eastern Washington University, Fisheries Technical Report No. 37, 108 p.

Matt, V.J., and Buchanan, J.P., 1993b, Drainage basin hydrology and geomorphology on the Spokane Indian Reservation: Upper Columbia United Tribes Fisheries Center, Eastern Washington University, Fisheries Technical Report No. 38, 93 p.

McLucas, G.B., 1980, Surficial geology of the Springdale and Forest Center quadrangles, Stevens County, Washington: Washington Division of Geology and Earth Resources Open-File Report 80-3, 29 p., 2 pls.

Molenaar, Dee, 1988, The Spokane aquifer, Washington— Its geologic origin and water-bearing and water-quality characteristics: U.S. Geological Survey Water-Supply Paper 2265, 74 p.

Muñoz-Villers, L.E., and López-Blanco, J., 2008, Land use/cover changes using Landsat TM/ETM images in a tropical and biodiverse mountainous area of central-eastern Mexico: International Journal of Remote Sensing, v. 29, no. 1, 71-93.

Multi-Resolution Land Characteristics Consortium, 2008, NLCD 2001 Land Cover Class Definitions, National Land Cover Database, accessed May 27, 2010, at http://www.mrlc.gov/nlcd_definitions.php.

National Geographic TOPO!,, 2007, Outdoor recreation mapping, Washington, version 4.2.8, 5: National Geographic software, compact discs.

Oregon State University, 2010, Oregon Climate Service: Corvallis, Oregon State University, College of Oceanic and Atmospheric Sciences website, accessed March 22, 2010, at http://www.ocs.oregonstate.edu/index html.

Peone, R., Scholz, A., Doughtie, C., and Kube, H., 1993, An inventory of surface water and groundwater resources on the Spokane Indian Reservation, including identification of factors with potential to impact water quality, utilizing geographic information system (GIS) mapping: Wellpinit, Wash., Spokane Tribal Fish and Wildlife Center, and Upper Columbia United Tribes Fisheries Center, Eastern Washington University, Fisheries Technical Report No. 42, 100 p.

Richmond, G.M., Fryxell, R., Neff, G.E., and Weis, P.L., 1965, The Cordilleran ice sheet of the northern Rocky Mountains, and the related Quaternary history of the Columbia Plateau, in Wright, H.E., Jr., and Frey, D.G., eds., The Quaternary of the United States: Princeton, N.J., Princeton University Press, p. 231-242.

Rittenhouse-Zeman and Associates, Inc., 1989, Well construction and aquifer testing, Deep aquifer at Galbraith Springs, Stevens County, Washington: Beaverton, Oreg., Rittenhouse-Zeman and Associates [variously paged].

Stevens County Assessor, 2010, Parcel Data Base Information System and Assessor's Maps, accessed November 12, 2007 at http://www.co.stevens.wa.us/assessor/RealProp/real property_search_assessor.htm.

Stoffel, K.L., Joseph, N.L., Waggoner, S.Z., Gulick, C.W., Korosec, M.A., and Bunning, B.B., 1991, Geologic map of Washington northeast quadrant: Washington Division of Geology and Earth Resources, Geologic map GM-39, scale 1:250,000.

Tetra Tech/KLM, 2007, Water Resource Inventory Area 54 (Lower Spokane) watershed plan, Phase 2, Level 1 Technical Assessment: Spokane County database, accessed August 2008 at http://www.spokanecounty.org/wqmp/project54/ASP/P2L1TechAssmnt_index.asp.

U.S. Geological Survey, 2007, Water resources of the United States, 2007: U. S. Geological Survey Water-Resources Data Report. (Available at http://wdr.water.usgs.gov/wy2007/search.jsp).

U.S. Geological Survey, 2008, Water resources of the United States, 2008: U. S. Geological Survey Water-Resources Data Report. (Available at http://wdr.water.usgs.gov/wy2008/search.jsp).

U.S. Geological Survey, 2009, Earth Resources and Science (EROS) Center Thematic Mapper (TM), Products and Data: U.S. Geological Survey database, available at http://eros.usgs.gov/#/Find_Data/Products_and_Data_Available/TM.

Waitt, R.B., Jr., 1980, About forty last-glacial Lake Missoula jökulhlaups through southern Washington: Journal of Geology, v. 88, p. 653-679.

Waitt, R.B., Jr., and Thorson R.M., 1983, The Cordilleran ice sheet in Washington, Idaho, and Montana, *in* Wright, H.E., and Porter, S.C., eds., Late-Quaternary environments of the United States, v. 1: Minneapolis, University of Minnesota Press, p. 53-70.

Washington Division of Geology and Earth Resources, 2005, Digital 1:100,000-scale geology of Washington State, version 1.0: Washington Division of Geology and Earth Resources Open-File Report 2005-3, accessed November 12, 2007 at http://www.dnr.wa.gov/ResearchScience/Topics/GeosciencesData/Pages/gis_data.aspx.

Washington State Department of Ecology, 2006, Water Resources Program – Water Rights, accessed August 22, 2006, at http://www.ecy.wa.gov/programs/wr/rights/water-right-home.html.

Washington State Department of Health, Division of Radiation Protection, 1991, Final environmental impact statement—Closure of the Dawn Mining Company uranium millsite in Ford, Washington: Olympia, Washington State Department of Health, 3 vol., variously paged.

Washington State Office of Financial Management, 2000, Census TIGER/Line File Extracts: Olympia, Washington State Office of Financial Management, accessed August 1, 2007, at Washington State Office of Financial Management (accessed August 2007 at http://www.ofm.wa.gov/pop/geographic/00tiger.asp).

Western Regional Climate Center, 2010, Western U.S. climate historical summary for Wellpinit, Washington: Western Regional Climate Center database, accessed January 6, 2010, at http://www.wrcc.dri.edu/cgi-bin/cliMAIN.pl?wa9058.

Whiteman, K.J., Vaccaro, J.J., Gonthier, J.B., and Bauer, H.H., 1994, The hydrogeologic framework and geochemistry of the Columbia Plateau aquifer system, Washington, Oregon, and Idaho: U.S. Geological Survey Professional Paper 1413-B, 73 p.

Willis, B., 1887, Changes in river courses in Washington Territory due to glaciation: U.S. Geological Survey Bulletin 40, p. 477-480.

Wozniewicz, J.V., 1989, Hydrogeology of the Chamokane valley aquifer system: Cheney, Eastern Washington University, Master of Science thesis, 172 p.

Appendix A.   Land Use and Land Cover Change Analysis

A land use and land cover (LULC) change analysis was done to supplement the understanding of the groundwater and surface-water system of the Chamokane Creek basin. Changes in land use and land cover can result in changes in recharge to the groundwater system and changes in how water is used in the basin. The term *land cover* refers to the physical attributes present on the surface of the Earth, and the term *land use* describes how a specific piece of land is used by humans (Lillesand and others, 2008). For some classes, these concepts are directly related. LULC change in the Chamokane Creek basin was assessed using satellite imagery.

Satellite images commonly are used to analyze LULC changes because they can provide extensive information for a specific period in a cost-effective method (Güler and others, 2007). Furthermore, satellites provide global and frequent coverage of the Earth and the data are readily accessible online. Images often are available in user-ready digital formats, which allow for quick access to time series data.

Although LULC data covering the Chamokane Creek basin study area are available (for example, Landscape Fire and Resource Management Planning Tools Project and the National Land Cover Database (Multi-Resolution Land Characteristics Consortium, 2008)), these generalized, national land cover products provide data only for select periods and usually are limited to recent years. It was not possible, therefore, to use currently available classification products for the LULC change analysis. Classifications specific to, or close to, the dates of interest (prior to the 1979 Adjudication and current (2009)) were needed. Furthermore, the classifications done specifically for this study are at a finer resolution than many of the National land cover products.

Methods

Data Acquisition

Landsat Thematic Mapper (TM) data were used for this study due to the availability of historical and continuous imagery. TM sensors on Landsat satellites have been collecting data since 1982. The TM sensor collects data in seven wavelength bands (six in the visible through mid-infrared regions of the electromagnetic spectrum and one thermal band) (Lillesand and others, 2008). TM data have a pixel size of 30 m (120 m for the thermal band). Landsat TM data were acquired from the U.S. Geological Survey Earth Resources Observation and Science Center (EROS, http:// glovis.usgs.gov/).

The Chamokane Creek basin study area is in path 43 and row 27 of the Worldwide Reference System-2, a cataloging system for Landsat data (fig. A1). The final dates selected for the LULC change analysis were October 11, 1987, and July 3, 2009. Landsat TM data from EROS generally is available for this location every 16 days. Some images were unusable due to heavy cloud cover. High quality images with minimal cloud cover were not available until July 1984. Orthophotos for the entire Chamokane Creek basin, however, were available starting in 1987. Orthophotos are aerial photographs that have been georectified and do not contain the distortions present in normal aerial photographs. Therefore, distances, angles, and areas may be measured directly from the photographs (Lillesand and others, 2008). Orthophotos of the study area were needed to conduct an accuracy assessment of the 1987 LULC classification. Although using data from the same season is often desirable in a LULC change analysis, high quality satellite images were not available until October 1987.

Data prior to adjudication (1979) would have been ideal for this analysis. However, the only satellite sensor dating back far enough is the Multispectral Scanner (MSS). Although MSS data are available as of 1972, images are of relatively low resolution (80 m) and are available only until 1992.

Image Classification and Change Analysis

A common approach to analyzing LULC data is to independently classify images from different periods and compare the images after classification to determine where changes on the landscape have occurred (Güler and others, 2006; Muñoz-Villers and López-Blanco, 2008).

To classify LULC for the historical (1987) and current (2009) images, a hybrid approach to image classification using ERDAS IMAGINE software was used. The hybrid approach incorporates two types of classifications: (1) unsupervised classification (program groups together pixels that are spectrally similar without any input from the user) and (2) supervised classification (user inputs a spectral signature file that the program uses to classify pixels). Prior to classification, selected images for each date were preprocessed by EROS with the Standard Terrain Correction (Level 1T), which provides systematic radiometric as well as geometric accuracy using ground control points and a DEM (U.S. Geological Survey, 2009).

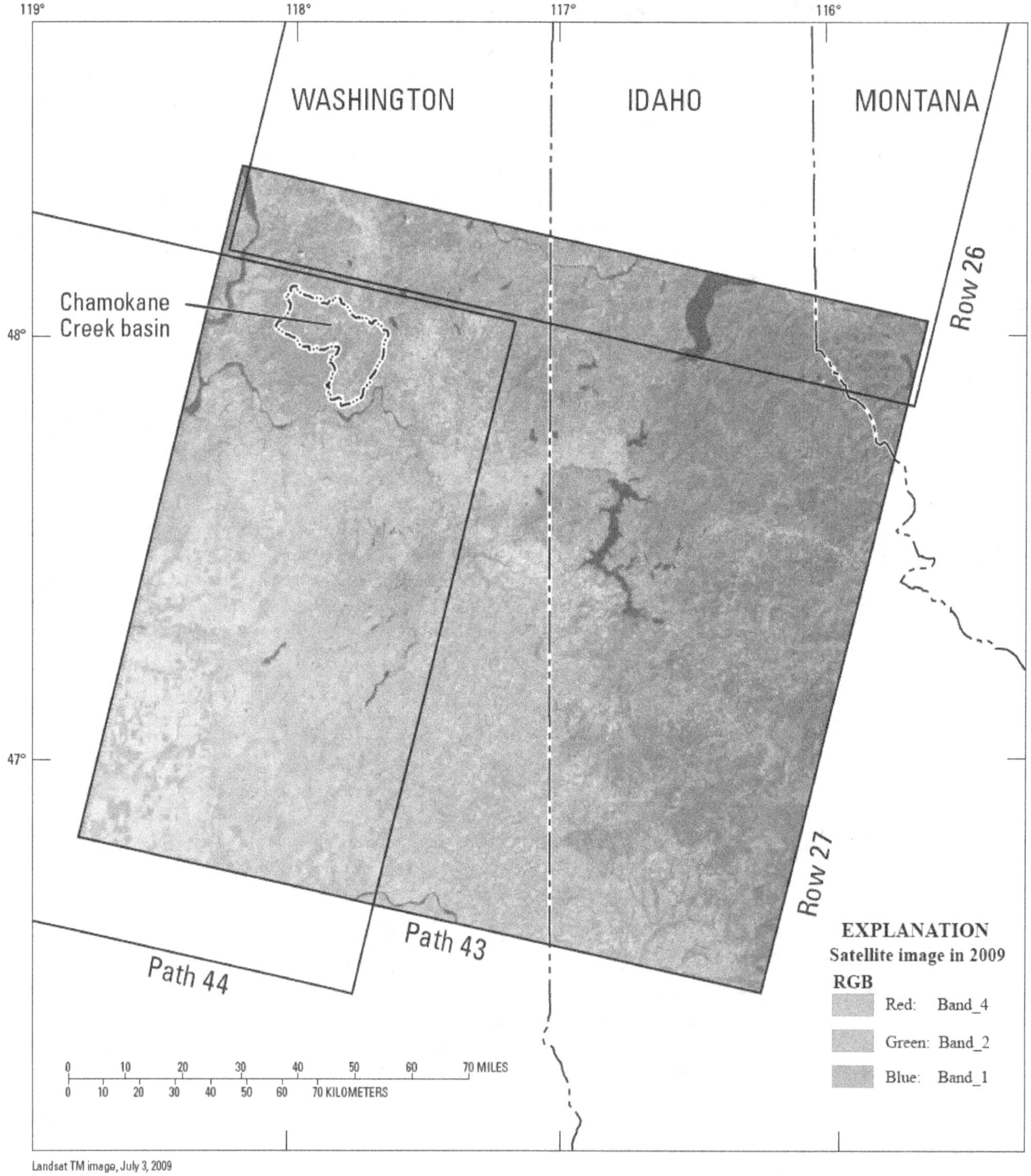

Landsat TM image, July 3, 2009

Figure A1.   Landsat Thematic Mapper image, July 3, 2009, (path 43, row 27), Chamokane Creek basin, Stevens County, Washington.

Landsat TM data for the two dates were independently classified. For each image, three main "image blocks" were created to represent the three major thematic materials in the scene; this method best captures the spectral variation within each theme. In this case, the selected themes were "forest," "agriculture," and "developed." Using an unsupervised classification, the program sorts pixels into a specific number of clusters based on their spectral signatures. The algorithm determines a mean signature for each cluster. Each cluster class is given a name based on reflectance values, known features, and other external information. These names and their corresponding signatures then were saved in a signature file. An unsupervised classification was carried out for each image block.

If more accurate data regarding land cover were available, these data were used to create training areas to assign a spectral signature to a known land cover type in the image. Supervised training areas were created from pixels of obvious or known features such as roads, water, and forest, from training data collected in the field, or from outside information such as the Washington State Department of Agriculture Crop Geodatabases. For each image block previously mentioned, the signature file from the unsupervised classification was edited to include spectral signatures of these known surface materials.

Once a spectral signature file for each image block was edited, all three image block files were merged into one master signature file. This file then was used to do a supervised classification on the entire image. In the supervised classification, each pixel was assigned to one of the signatures from the master signature file based on a maximum likelihood classifier algorithm. The classified images were smoothed with a majority filter using a 3×3 pixel moving window to reduce the number of misclassified pixels (Lillesand and others, 2008).

Once both images were classified, a pixel-by-pixel overlay procedure (Muñoz-Villers and López-Blanco, 2008) was carried out using ArcGIS to examine changes between the 1987 and 2009 LULC. A change map was created to examine the nature of the changes that occurred during this period.

Accuracy Assessment

To assess the accuracy of the 1987 classified image, 250 reference points were selected from historical 1987 orthophotos at a scale of 1:63,360 obtained from the Washington Department of Natural Resources. These points were selected based on a stratified random sampling design (except for water, which occurred only once in the classified image and, therefore, was only sampled once). To assess the accuracy of the 2009 classified image, 129 ground points in the study area were visited at the end of July 2009 (after the satellite image was taken). Due to limited access to

privately-owned lands, however, a random sampling method for selecting reference points was not possible for the 2009 image. Instead, reference points were taken systematically (every few miles) along as many roads as possible throughout the basin.

Classification accuracy was then evaluated using error matrices. The overall accuracy and the Khat statistic (KAPPA analysis) were computed to describe the accuracy of each classification. Differences in these two values were expected as the *overall accuracy* is simply the total number of correctly classified pixels divided by the total number of reference pixels, whereas the *Khat statistic* includes the errors of commission and omission, thereby indicating the extent to which the percentage of correct values in an error matrix are due to "true" versus "chance" agreement (Lillesand and others, 2008). The accuracies of users and producers also were calculated. User accuracy refers to the probability that a pixel is correctly classified by the user (or in historical orthophotos) and is a measure of commission error. Producer accuracy refers to the probability that reference pixels were correctly classified and is a measure of omission error.

Results

Land Use and Land Cover Classes

Seven LULC classes were identified in the classification process. Many of the classifications used were based on categories from the National Land Cover Database.

Evergreen forest – Areas dominated by evergreen trees greater than 5 m tall.

Open forest – Areas of open, low-density evergreen trees greater than 5 m tall. These areas may be naturally open ponderosa pine forests or low-density forests resulting from harvesting activities.

Shrub – Areas dominated by shrubs less than 5 m tall. Includes true shrubs as well as young trees in an early successional stage.

Grassland – Areas covered by grasses and other herbaceous vegetation. These areas are not subject to intensive management activities, but may be used for grazing.

Agriculture – Land that is used for the production of crops and is being actively tilled. Also includes pastures planted for livestock grazing.

Developed/Sparsely vegetated – Areas where there is little vegetation due to the presence of constructed materials, impervious surfaces, bare/barren land or clearcuts.

Water – Areas of open water.

Accuracy of Multispectral Analysis

The 1987 LULC map (fig. A2) has an overall accuracy of 86.5 percent and a Kappa index of agreement of 0.83. The error matrix containing user and producer accuracies for 1987 is shown in table A1. The accuracy of producers was greater than 80 percent for all classes except "developed/sparsely vegetated." Only 63.0 percent of areas that are developed/sparsely vegetated were correctly identified. However, 85.0 percent of areas classified as developed/sparsely vegetated were in this class. It appears that some developed/sparsely vegetated areas were classified incorrectly as either grassland or agriculture. The accuracy of users was greater than 80 percent for all classes except "open forest" and "grassland." Although 90.6 percent of areas with open forest cover were correctly identified by producers as open forest, only 78.4 percent of areas classified by users as open forest actually were in that category. Some areas with evergreen forest cover, shrub cover, or grassland cover were classified as open forest. Similarly, although 81.3 percent of grasslands were correctly identified by producers, only 66.7 percent of areas classified by users as grasslands are actually in that category. This is mainly because developed/sparsely vegetated areas were misclassified as grassland. Some agricultural and open forest areas also were misclassified as grassland.

The 2009 LULC map (fig. A3) has an overall accuracy of 90.7 percent with a Kappa index of agreement of 0.89. The accuracy was greater than 80 percent for all classes except developed/sparsely vegetated (table A2). Only 73.3 percent of developed/sparsely vegetated areas were correctly identified by producers . However, 84.6 percent of areas identified as developed/sparsely vegetated by users actually were in this class. Some developed/sparsely vegetated areas are being classified incorrectly as agriculture or water. The accuracy of the users was greater than 80 percent for all classes except open forest and water. Although 100 percent of areas with open forest cover were correctly identified as such, only 78.9 percent of areas classified as open forest were actually in that category. Areas covered in shrubs, grassland, or agriculture also were included in the open forest category.

Land Use and Land Cover Change Analysis

Forest cover is the dominant land cover type in the Chamokane Creek basin. The area distribution for classes in 1987 and 2009 as well as the change in area of each class is presented in table A3. Areas that have changed in classification during this period and which classifications they changed to are shown in figures A4 and A5.

In 1987, evergreen forests covered 65.4 percent of the area in the basin. This does not include ponderosa pine forests, however, which are in the southern part of the basin. Ponderosa pine forests are naturally open, park-like forests that are spectrally similar to forests with a low density of trees from logging activities. Therefore, these two forest types were identified as a single class "open forest." It is reasonable to assume that areas classified as "open forest" in the upper part of the basin are due to logging activities, whereas areas classified as "open forest" in the lower part of the basin are naturally open ponderosa pine forests. In 2009, evergreen forest covered 55.9 percent of the basin. Once again, this does not include ponderosa pine forests and likely is an underestimate of total natural forest cover in the basin.

Between 1987 and 2009, evergreen forest cover decreased by nearly 11,000 acres, or 14.5 percent of the original forest cover. Much of this decrease was a result of a change in classification of 9,800 acres of evergreen forest to open forest. Additionally, 5,300 acres of evergreen forest became shrub, 2,300 acres became grassland and 1,300 acres became developed/sparsely vegetated. Major changes in land cover *to* the evergreen forest category include 1,800 acres of grassland, 4,900 acres of shrub, and 740 acres of open forest. Therefore, net changes of evergreen forest to shrub and evergreen forest to grassland were relatively small (less than about 500 acres).

Open forest cover increased from 6.97 to 17.4 percent of the total basin area (an increase of more than 12,000 acres). Other major changes include about 1,800 acres of grassland, 1,600 acres of shrub, and 1,800 acres of agriculture becoming open forest in 2009. About 1,800 acres of open forest changed in classification to grassland so the net change between open forest and grassland was minor. About 740 acres of open forest changed to evergreen forest.

Although the overall area of shrub cover has remained relatively stable (about 8 percent of total land area), various spatial changes from and to this category occurred. About 4,900 acres changed in classification from shrub to evergreen forest, 1,600 acres changed from shrub to open forest, and 1,100 acres changed from shrub to grassland. Additionally, about 5,300 acres changed from evergreen forest to shrub and 1,000 acres changed from agriculture to shrub.

Between 1987 and 2009, areas classified as grassland increased from 6.56 percent of the total basin area (about 7,600 acres) to 10.3 percent (about 12,000 acres). The greatest change in this category came from 3,900 acres of agriculture becoming grassland, in addition to the changes to grassland mentioned previously. This change from agriculture to grassland has largely effected the total amount of agriculture in the basin, which has decreased by approximately one-half, from 10.9 to 5.3 percent of the total basin area. Changes in classification from agriculture to shrub and open forest also have noticeably decreased the amount of land classified as agriculture.

Developed/sparsely vegetated areas make up a small percentage of the total basin. Only 1.71 percent of the total basin area (almost 2,000 acres) was classified under this category in 1987, increasing to 2.8 percent (almost 3,300 acres) in 2009. This increase came from areas previously classified as evergreen forest. Finally, areas classified as water increased by a magnitude of 10, although water was less than 0.5 percent of the total basin area.

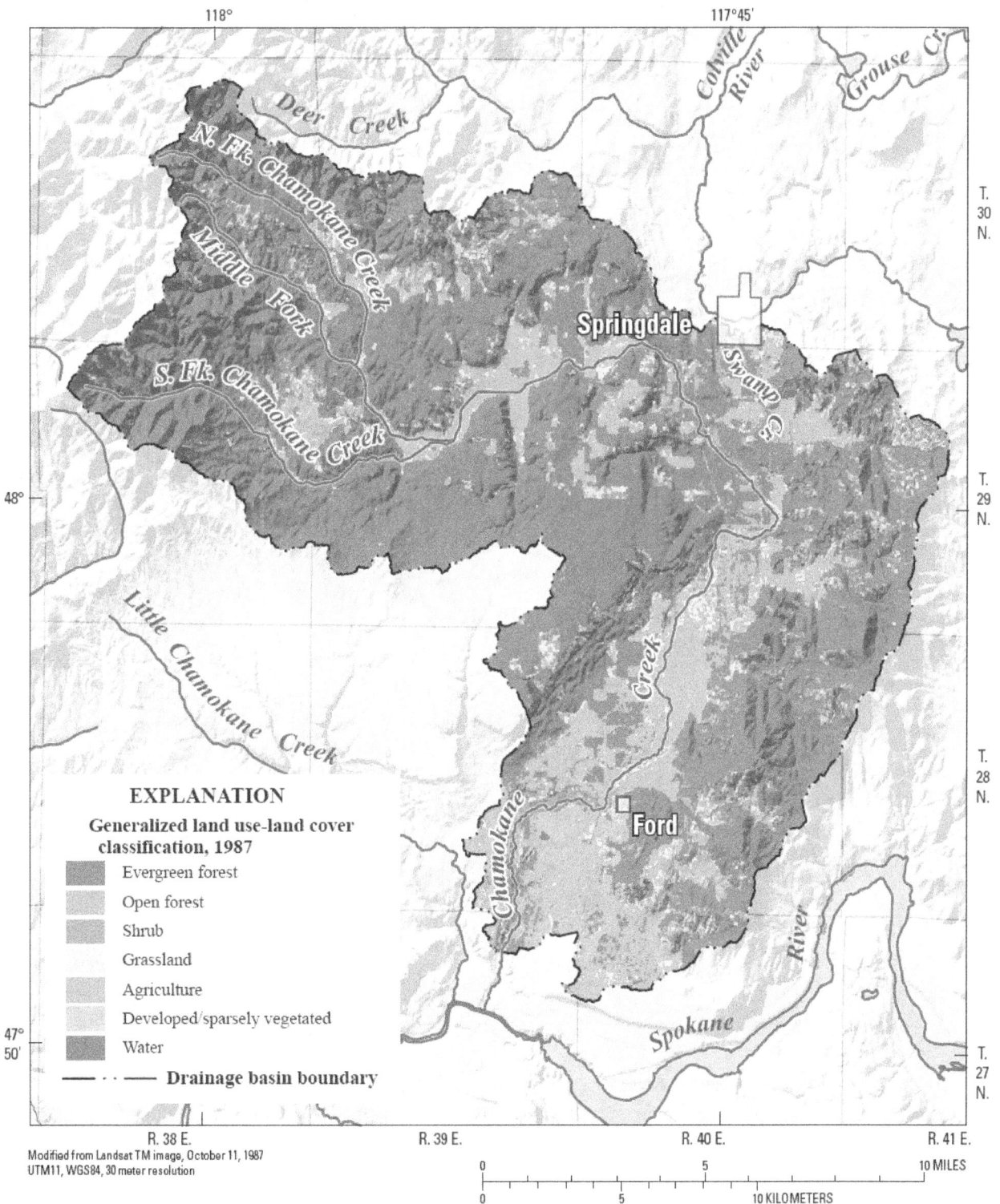

Figure A2.   Map showing generalized land use and land cover classification for 1987, Chamokane Creek basin, Stevens County, Washington.

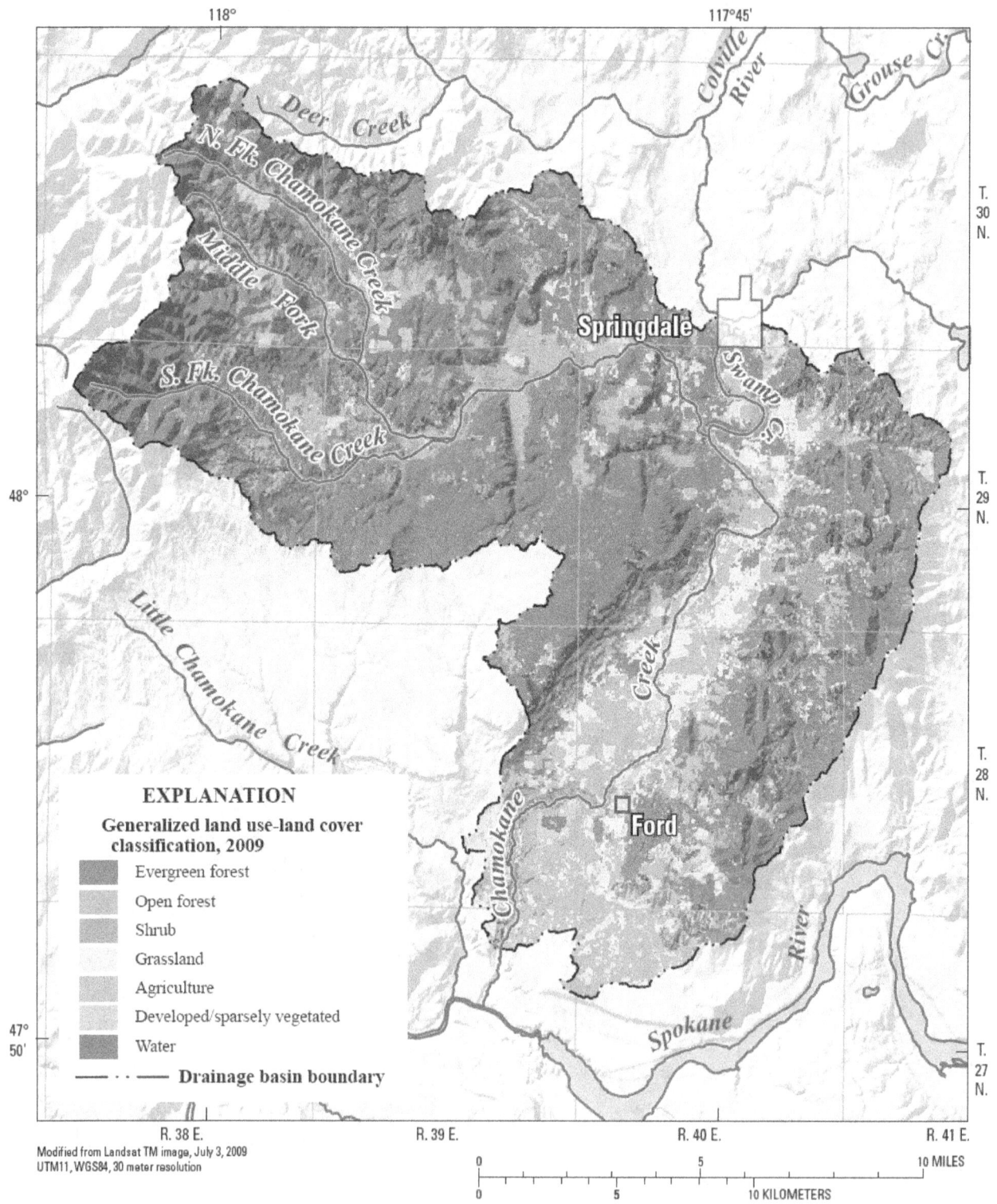

Figure A3.   Map showing generalized land use and land cover classification for 2009, Chamokane Creek basin, Stevens County, Washington.

Table A1.   Error matrix for 1987 Landsat Thematic Mapper classified image of Chamokane Creek basin, Stevens County, Washington.

1987 Landsat TM classified data	1987 Orthophoto reference data							Row total	User accuracy (percent)
	Evergreen forest	Open forest	Shrub	Grassland	Agriculture	Developed/ sparsely vegetated	Water		
Evergreen forest	82							82	100.0
Open forest	4	29	2	2				37	78.4
Shrub	2		31	1				34	91.2
Grassland		3	1	26	3	6		39	66.7
Agriculture	1			2	31	4		38	81.6
Developed/sparsely vegetated				1	2	17		20	85.0
Water							1	1	100.0
Column total	89	32	34	32	36	27	1	251	
Producer's accuracy (percent)	92.1	90.6	91.2	81.3	86.1	63.0	100.0		

Table A2.   Error matrix for 2009 Landsat Thematic Mapper classified image of Chamokane Creek basin, Stevens County, Washington.

2009 Landsat TM classified data	2009 Ground reference data							Row total	User accuracy (percent)
	Evergreen forest	Open forest	Shrub	Grassland	Agriculture	Developed/ sparsely vegetated	Water		
Evergreen forest	26							26	100.0
Open forest		15	1	1	2			19	78.9
Shrub			10					10	100.0
Grassland				26	1			27	96.3
Agriculture				1	26	3		30	86.7
Developed/sparsely vegetated				1	1	11		13	84.6
Water						1	3	4	75.0
Column total	26	15	11	29	30	15	3	129	
Producer's accuracy (percent)	100.0	100.0	90.9	89.7	86.7	73.3	100.0		

Table A3.   Comparison of acreages by class for land use and land cover classifications and change in acreage between 1987 and 2009, Chamokane Creek basin, Stevens County, Washington.

Class	1987		2009		1987–2009
	Area		Area		Change in area
	Acres	Percent	Acres	Percent	Acres
Evergreen forest	75,809.7	65.4	64,824.5	55.9	-10,985.2
Open forest	8,077.2	6.97	20,195.4	17.4	12,118.3
Shrub	9,738.9	8.41	9,317.7	8.0	-421.2
Grassland	7,601.9	6.56	11,948.2	10.3	4,346.3
Agriculture	12,631.8	10.9	6,115.9	5.3	-6,515.9
Developed/sparsely vegetated	1,986.4	1.71	3,281.4	2.8	1,295.0
Water	18.0	0.02	180.8	0.2	162.8
Total	115,863.9	100	115,863.9	100	

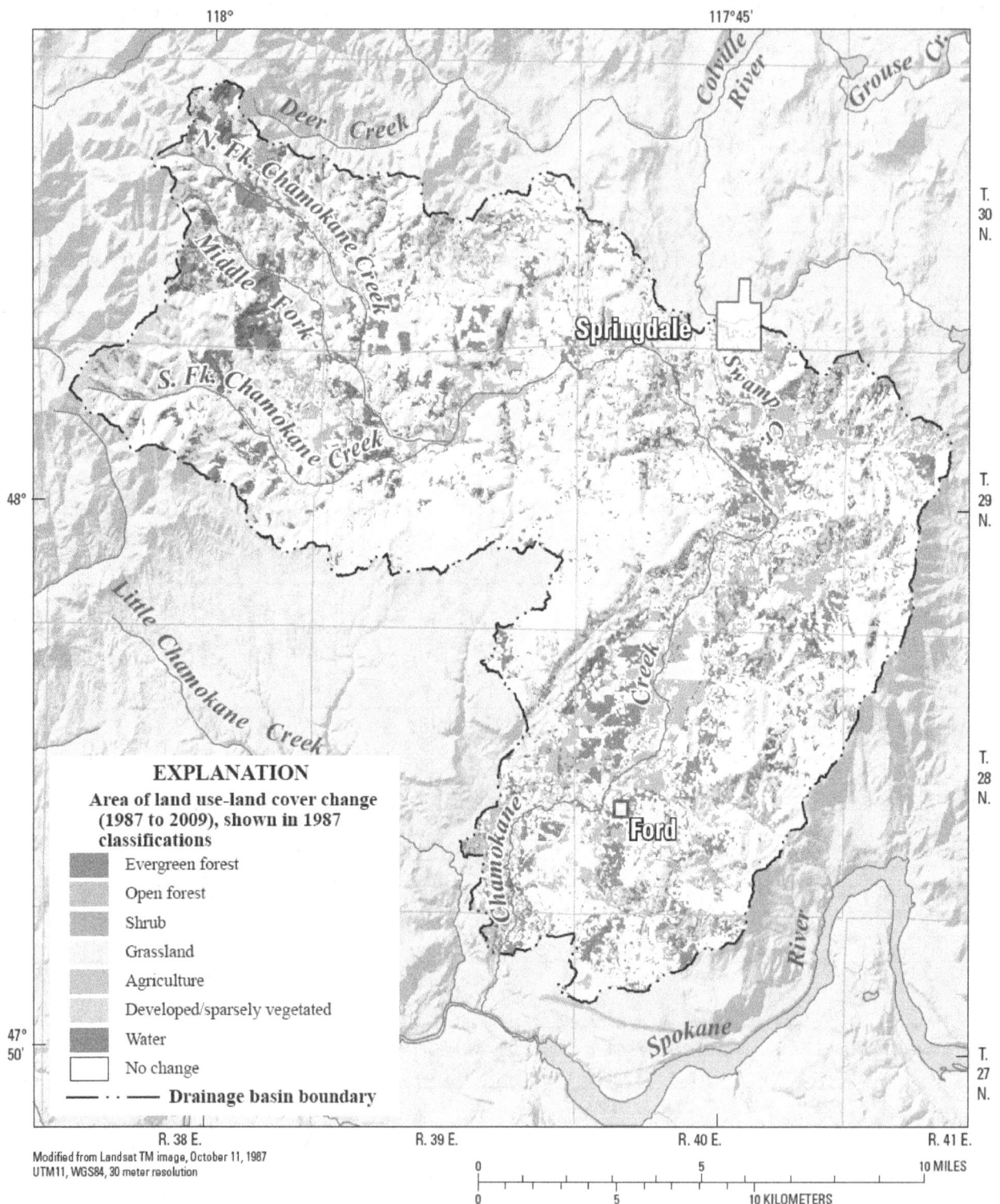

Modified from Landsat TM image, October 11, 1987
UTM11, WGS84, 30 meter resolution

Figure A4.   Map showing land use and land cover classification changes from 1987 to 2009, (1987 classifications that changed), Chamokane Creek basin, Stevens County, Washington.

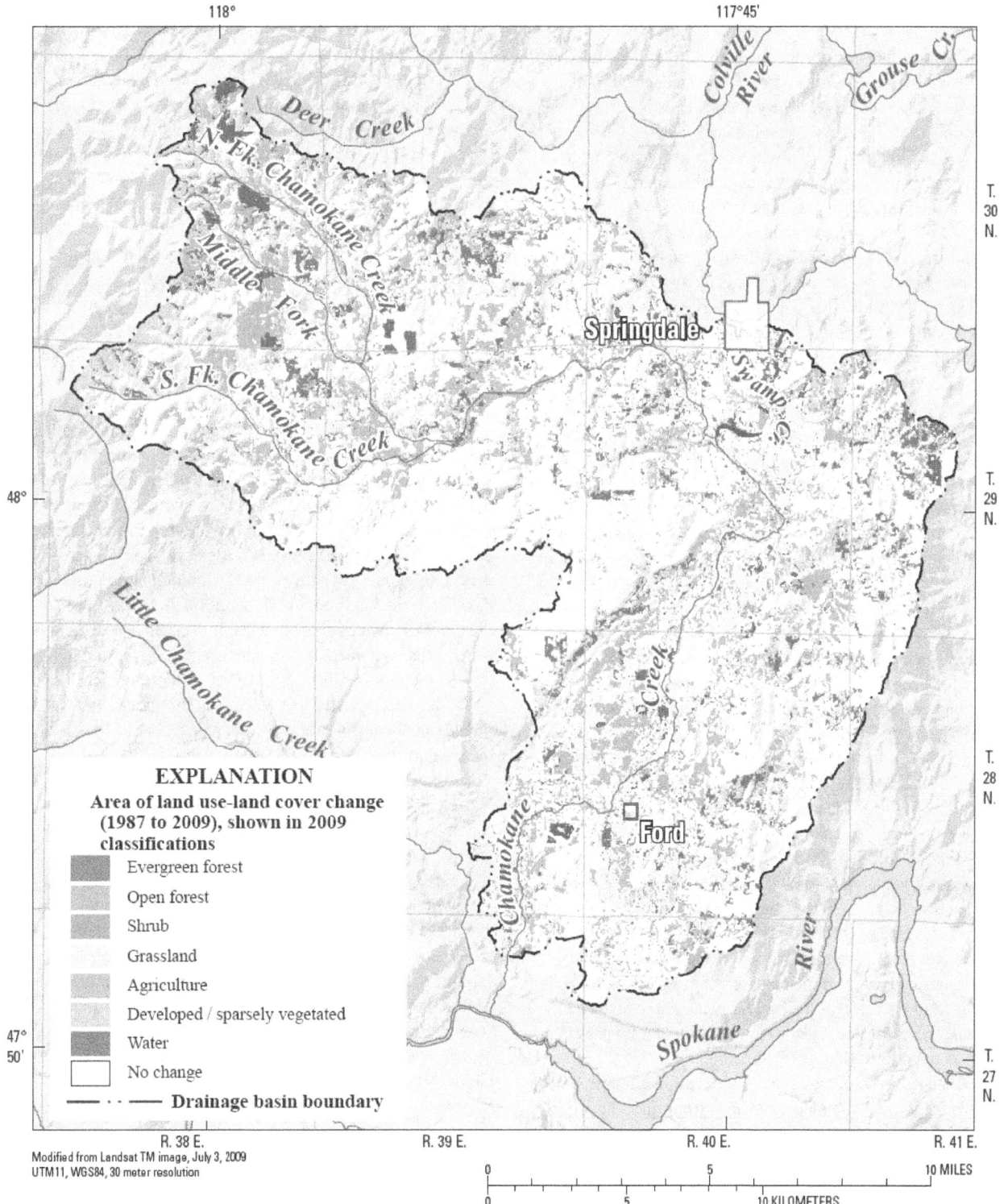

Figure A5. Map showing land use and land cover classification changes from 1987 to 2009, (2009 area classifications that changed), Chamokane Creek basin, Stevens County, Washington.

Discussion

Chamokane Creek basin currently (2009) is an area dominated by forests with some pasture and agricultural lands. Development is relatively sparse. Loss in forest cover represents the largest change in land cover in the basin between 1987 and 2009. This appears to be mostly due to forestry activities, especially in the northern part of the basin. Since 1987, more than 18,000 acres of evergreen forest have been logged and are at various stages of regrowth. Recently, 1,300 of these acres were harvested, falling under the classification of "developed/sparsely vegetated." Between 1987 and 2009, more than 7,000 acres of shrub, grassland and open forest have changed in classification to evergreen forest, indicating previously logged areas that have now regenerated.

Much of the increase in the open forest classification from 1987 to 2009 also is a result of harvesting practices. Areas likely are being converted from evergreen forest to low-density, open forests from logging activities. Although to a lesser extent, changes from evergreen forest to open forest also may be the result of development activities, especially in the corridor along State Route 231 that connects the towns of Ford and Springdale. Development occurs at such a small scale in the basin relative to the pixel size of the satellite sensors (30 m^2) that some development in this heavily forested area may be picked up as open forest rather than developed/sparsely vegetated. The accuracy of the developed/sparsely vegetated classification generally was not as high as in other classes. Similar issues occurred with the accuracy of classifying water due to the small scale and low number of water bodies in the basin.

According to the 2009 accuracy assessment, areas determined to be grassland, shrub, or agriculture were mistakenly classified as open forest. This may be due to confusion between spectral signatures. Areas that are mostly covered in grassland, shrub, or agriculture (pasture), but that also have some trees, may at times appear like open forestland. Therefore, some of the changes from these categories in 1987 *to* the open forest category may not represent actual changes. Similarly, changes *from* the open forest category to the grassland or evergreen forest category also may be inaccurate, because there was some error in classifying these land cover types as open forest in the 1987 image.

Changes in shrub cover mainly occurred on lands where forestry activities took place. Changes from shrub cover, specifically of young evergreen trees, to forest cover likely are a result of regeneration, and changes from forest cover to shrub are due to more recent logging activities, where regeneration is ongoing.

Changes that involve deciduous shrub cover, grasslands, and agricultural lands are difficult to analyze because the 1987 image was taken in autumn and the 2009 image was taken in summer. The difference in seasons of the two images may influence the LULC classifications, with deciduous plants looking vastly different between the summer and autumn, herbaceous plants dying back at the end of the growing season, and crops drying and being harvested at various points in time. Furthermore, although it appears that there has been a substantial decrease in the amount of agricultural lands and increase in the amount of grasslands in the basin, this could be a hasty conclusion and additional investigation is necessary to make this determination. The agriculture class includes a diverse group of land cover types, which is not ideal for a spectral signature. In addition to various crop types, some areas (though not many) are irrigated, certain crops are cut multiple times and have variable densities, and some fields are fallow or have been recently harvested. Pastureland also may have been classified as agriculture in some areas and as grassland in other areas. Therefore, overlap between these two classes probably exists. Although agriculture may have decreased in the basin, it is not likely to have been to the extent shown by this analysis. It is especially difficult to differentiate between classes such as agriculture and grassland from orthophotos. Changes in LULC often can occur rapidly due to harvesting activities; what was captured by the satellite image may be different from what is seen in orthophotos or on the ground.

This analysis highlighted major changes that occurred in the Chamokane Creek basin between 1987 and 2009, specifically regarding evergreen forest cover. The analysis also will provide more specific LULC data for GSFLOW model compared to the generalized LULC products that currently are available. Additional studies would be needed to answer questions regarding changes in agriculture and specific crop types as well as changes in developed land area. Newer satellite sensors can show much more detail about present-day LULC; however, information regarding historical LULC will remain quite coarse. Further processing of the images and more advanced classification programs (for example, feature-based) also could help refine the LULC classifications for Chamokane Creek basin.

References Cited in Appendix A

Güler, Mustafa, Yomralioğlu Tahsin, and Reis, Selçuk 2007, Using landsat data to determine land use/land cover changes in Samsun, Turkey: Environmental Monitoring and Assessment, v. 127, no. 1–3, p. 113.

Lillesand, T. M., Kiefer, R.W., and W. Chipman, J.W., 2008, Remote sensing and image interpretation: Hoboken, N.J., John Wiley & Sons, 736 p.

Muñoz-Villers, L.E., and López-Blanco, J., 2008, Land use/cover changes using Landsat TM/ETM images in a tropical and biodiverse mountainous area of central-eastern Mexico: International Journal of Remote Sensing, v. 29, no. 1, 71-93.

Multi-Resolution Land Characteristics Consortium, 2008, NLCD 2001 Land Cover Class Definitions, National Land Cover Database, accessed May 27, 2010, at http://www.mrlc.gov/nlcd_definitions.php.

U.S. Geological Survey, 2009, Earth Resources and Science (EROS) Center Thematic Mapper (TM), Products and Data: U.S. Geological Survey database, available at http://eros.usgs.gov/#/Find_Data/Products_and_Data_Available/TM.